Very Special Maths

All children require mathematical understanding to access as full a life as possible. This practical book explores the curriculum required to accommodate the various difficulties faced by children with severe and profound learning difficulties. It describes how children's mathematical thinking first develops and how it can be nurtured to ensure real understanding and support essential life skills.

Chapters explore key concepts including:

- quantity recognition and counting

- sequence and measurement

- comparisons

- space and shape

- time

- monetary value.

Mindful of the diverse challenges faced by teachers and pupils, the book explains the neurological and pedagogical theories that underpin the development of early mathematical thinking. It considers how mathematical skills that will best support children's everyday functioning can be developed. Practical ideas and activities for application in the classroom are further supported by illustrative diagrams, case studies and detailed online reading to deepen teachers' understanding and confidence when working with pupils.

An essential and inspiring guide for teachers, special educational needs coordinators, teaching assistants, and parents, this text proves that with the appropriate strategies, each child is able to develop the mathematical skills essential to everyday living.

Les Staves has over 45 years of experience working within special education. He is recognised internationally as a freelance writer, consultant, and trainer.

Very Special Maths

Developing Thinking and Maths Skills for Pupils with Severe or Complex Learning Difficulties

Les Staves

Routledge
Taylor & Francis Group

LONDON AND NEW YORK

First published 2019
by Routledge
2 Park Square, Milton Park, Abingdon, Oxon OX14 4RN

and by Routledge
711 Third Avenue, New York, NY 10017

Routledge is an imprint of the Taylor & Francis Group, an informa business

British Library Cataloguing in Publication Data
A catalogue record for this book is available from the British Library

Library of Congress Cataloging in Publication Data
Names: Staves, Les, author.
Title: Very special maths : developing thinking and maths skills for pupils
with severe or complex learning difficulties / Les Staves.
Description: Abingdon, Oxon ; New York, NY : Routledge, 2019.
Identifiers: LCCN 2018009734 (print) | LCCN 2018016944 (ebook) |
ISBN 9781315638348 (eb) | ISBN 9781138195516 (hb) | ISBN 9781138195530 (pb)
Subjects: LCSH: Special education–Mathematics. | Mathematics–Study and
teaching. | Mathematics–Study and teaching–Activity programs. |
Learning disabled children–Education. | Children with disabilities–Education.
Classification: LCC QA11.2 (ebook) | LCC QA11.2 .S73 2019 (print) |
DDC 371.9/0447–dc23
LC record available at https://lccn.loc.gov/2018009734

ISBN: 978-1-138-19551-6 (hbk)
ISBN: 978-1-138-19553-0 (pbk)
ISBN: 978-1-315-63834-8 (ebk)

Typeset in Melior
by Out of House Publishing

Visit the eResources: www.routledge.com/9781138195530

Contents

Acknowledgements

I have worked with very special children since the inception of schools for them, and practice has changed radically. Along the way, the people who have influenced this book are many. There are those who are mentioned in the text for their thinking and practice, but there is also a legion of others. All the teachers, teaching assistants, parents and therapists I have worked with – they are a special community of remarkable commitment and I have to thank them all for what they have contributed to my knowledge, and all they do for special children.

Finally, those who have read and corrected my work so assiduously – good friend Keir Davidson and patient wife Wendy Headley.

About the author

Les Staves has worked with children with very special needs in the UK since 1973. As a classroom teacher, he was an early exponent of interactive sensory approaches when special education was in a pioneering phase. Later, he was head teacher of an outstanding special school. As a consultant and author, he has written materials for children with special educational needs that were distributed into schools by UK government bodies and other national agencies. Since his first book in 2000, his writings and training have influenced practical approaches to the special education of children with severe or profound learning difficulties in the UK and abroad.

Part I

About a special curriculum

What this book is about

Teaching very special mathematics and thinking

This book is about teaching children with very special educational needs who continue to work at early levels of learning throughout their school careers – or lives. Mostly it is about children who work below the levels described by the National Curriculum. Some will be unable to count, many will not be fluent, some will use small counting practically and some will seem to count well – but do not understand what they are doing. So what *is* mathematics for these children? Is it relevant to teach them? I hope to make you think positively and help you teach them useful skills – including 'thinking'.

The book refers to the very wide range of children across all age phases and settings of special education. These children have so many different characteristics that there will inevitably be generalisations or places where points only apply to particular groups.

The usual labels applied in the UK to these children describe two broad groups with 'severe' or 'profound' learning difficulties – using acronyms of SLD and PLD – and both groups include *some* who are on the autistic spectrum. Some schools also have children with moderate learning difficulties or SLD pupils who progress and reach the early levels of the National Curriculum, so some of the book is about children who are beginning to be numerate.

Throughout the book, I often refer to the children as 'special', or 'very special', simply because firstly it is positive and that is how I see the characters that I have spent a lifetime teaching. Their learning processes and personalities have fascinated and taught me. Their progress has given me joy, and I have known heartache with them, too. Secondly, I refer to them in that way to avoid too much repetition of acronyms and long clinical descriptions.

 1.1 See online reading for an overview of very special children

A time of change

We are at an exciting time. Curriculum structures are changing, and many schools may elect to use 'life skills' or 'thinking skills' as the themes of their curriculum frameworks, whilst others may retain some subject teaching, including maths.

Whatever curriculum model we adopt, a purpose of our teaching must be to enable these children to access as full a life as possible. Maths comes into it because there are so many ways that they need to understand about all sorts of things such as the quantities, sequences, comparisons of spaces and shapes they use and the time they live through. They need practical understanding of how changes affect them and how they can affect changes. That is the kind of mathematics that is essential to them as they deal with everyday living. So, in this book, I will explore how children learn about these things. This book will be useful for teachers, whichever curriculum model they work with. I will try to illustrate how maths can be practical or social or cultural – and illustrate the learning processes that are needed within a practical curriculum.

2 About curriculum attitudes and mindsets

About curriculum attitudes

Before 1970, the children this book is about had no right to education and there were no schools for them. When the schools were opened our curriculum ambitions were only practical and influenced by negative ideas about these children's potential. The introduction of the National Curriculum forced changes. At our best, creative teachers radically interpreted subject content into creative teaching that inspired pupils to new learning – you can read about inspirational teachers in the online files. But this approach also sometimes sank into tokenism or teaching inappropriate subject content. Worst of all, there was pressure to measure children's progress with unsuitable measures, and too often assessment dominated thinking about the nature of what should be taught.

Now there is a time of change. More schools are evolving the ways they teach, and at the forefront of their minds is that their curriculum should outline teaching that is engaging and appropriate.

 2.1 See online reading for more about the background to development – and different curriculum perspectives

Mindsets

Our mindset about maths

The purpose of this book is to explore creative ways of developing the roots of practical mathematical thinking and activity for very special children. The trouble with maths is that many people are anxious about it, remembering it as something they didn't like at school. Maths anxiety is an affliction that many of us share and, if the number of people who deny being *good* at maths is anything to go by, there is even the possibility we are a majority – and this in turn might affect the value we put on maths or the roles we attribute to it as an element of a relevant curriculum for children with very special needs.

Is maths an abstract subject?

If people think that maths is an abstract subject that begins with counting and is all about juggling numbers and getting answers correct, or naming and theorising about shapes, they are likely to have a negative attitude towards its relevance for pupils who work at very early cognitive levels. By extension, they may also think of these children as being people who cannot benefit from that aspect of culture. Sadly, the belief that 'they can't count so maths is irrelevant' is not uncommon, and is an idea that potentially opens doors to other negative attitudes. The roots of mathematics are essential parts of our social lives long before we can count. Whilst it is true that the programmes of the conventional curriculum being written for the typical majority of children at school age do not begin at the beginning of life learning – and so do not match the needs of our special pupils – there is still a huge root system of pre-numerate learning that is usually developed before school age, which *is* relevant – it is the roots of life maths.

Our mindset about pupils

Through the sway of their expectations, teachers can be either the greatest asset or a negative influence on children's lives. If our curriculum philosophy begins by thinking about what children *cannot achieve*, we run the risk of limiting both our ambition for them and their potential. We have to ask – are there curriculum attitudes that can incorporate both realism and positive outlooks?

Even for our most profoundly disabled students, we must want to seek to expand their capability to interact socially. The online reading includes an example of how our attitudes and ideas about the relevance of exploration have changed. Promoting curiosity and the urge to solve the immediate problems that they face is the root of thinking – the seedbed of communication – and almost always includes elements of changing quantities, or space or time – the roots of life's maths.

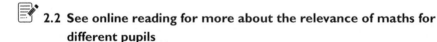 **2.2 See online reading for more about the relevance of maths for different pupils**

The mindset of this book

A basic premise in the book is that even though the National Curriculum does not begin at the beginning of mathematical learning, a curriculum for our very special pupils should seek to enable them to learn to think about the maths that is relevant for their lives.

Whether a school's curriculum incorporates subject teaching including maths or whether it is presented as 'life skills', 'thinking skills' or 'problem solving', it will contain learning that is related to mathematics, because mathematics is reflected and used in every physical, practical and cultural experience. So we need to know how children learn about quantities, changes, values, space and time.

Across this community of very special children, pupils access learning, that includes maths, at different levels:

1. *All children* begin at levels of gathering and applying sensory experience to developing the skills of 'learning to learn' and learning to live. These include aspects of development and learning to interact with their environment.

2. *Some pupils* will progress on a practical continuum from sensory learning towards appreciating the consequences of changes and thinking about them. Some begin to appreciate numerate levels. Teachers working with them need to understand how to develop practical ideas relating to quantity and number that are useful to life. Fundamental skills like itemising, comparing and matching, coordinated speech, etc., are life skills that contribute to thinking – and, for some children, work towards skills of counting.

3. *Still other pupils* will progress to practical or even abstract arithmetic, and for them we will need to know about how the 'big ideas' of maths grow.
   Some of these pupils will reach levels described by the National Curriculum, albeit at a later age than the programmes of study prescribe.

An image that the book will plant is that if we were to look upon the mainstream curriculum as a tree, a lot of the learning that would be most appropriate for our special pupils is the roots. For effective learning, those roots are important *to everybody*, but because they are also the essentials of social living and cultural experience, they are particularly relevant to our special pupils' life needs – and for this reason should form the basis of a curriculum. As far as numeracy goes, Farragher and Brown (2005)[1] remind us that numeracy for special pupils is a matter of quality of life.

Note

1 Farragher, R. & Brown, R. I. (2005) Numeracy for adults with Down syndrome: it's a matter of quality of life. *Journal of Intellectual Disability Research* 49(10), 761–5.

3 The place of maths in a very special curriculum

Why mathematics is important to special pupils

> The word 'math' is from Greek *mathema*, which means 'that which is learnt'. 'Matic' comes from *matos*, which means 'willing to [perform]'. Its original meaning comes from being 'willing to learn' – applied to anything.

This is appropriate to this book because I will argue that mathematics is everywhere and its processes are for learning about life.

There is a great deal of maths before the levels described by the National Curriculum. It is present in our earliest functions and the foundations of learning that spring from them and it continues to develop through everyday life. It has fundamental levels, where exploration leads to practical knowing and 'thinking'.

Over recent years, most special schools have provided adapted access to National Curriculum subjects, particularly Maths and English. Many are now looking away from being tied to 'subject' teaching and turning towards life skills, or using a developmental curriculum including communication and cognition. However they decide to arrange curriculum delivery, the children will need support with aspects of mathematical learning, because maths, in its widest senses and even at pre-numerate levels, is woven into every aspect of living – its patterns are within the forms of our thinking.

Mathematics is woven into living

It is part of development of thinking and reasoning.

- *In communications* about the nature of actions and order of things, it is in all descriptions of quantities, space and time.

- *In practical activity*, its concepts are the basis of all practical skills – making anything requires using maths.

- *Understanding relationships* – it is used to describe and compare things.

■ *Being systematic* – we use it to bring order, remember, predict, organise and record what has happened – or might happen.

■ *It is a tool for our imagination* – its patterns are part of music, movement, speech and the visual and tactile arts.

■ *It fascinates us* – even though many people are anxious about abstract mathematical language and processes, they are fascinated by comparisons and changes of quantities or sizes, frequencies, sequences and patterns of events, etc.

Maths supports the development of curiosity and enjoyment through its ability to describe patterns and all aspects of the world around us.

The following mind map illustrates that aspects of mathematical knowledge or skills occur in many parts our lives.

Mathematics occurs in all of these contexts:

■ Social activities and routines

■ Personal care routines

■ Domestic and practical activities

■ Participation in cultural activities

■ Participation in games

■ Creative expression

They all require:

■ Developing physical skills

■ Developing sequential skills and memory

■ Anticipating or predicting changes

■ Communicating about and affecting changes we observe or need

■ Absorbing a fund of knowledge

■ Making choices, or taking decisions, to solve problems

■ Working from practical towards more abstract thinking

So teaching these skills should be part of a maths curriculum for very special children.

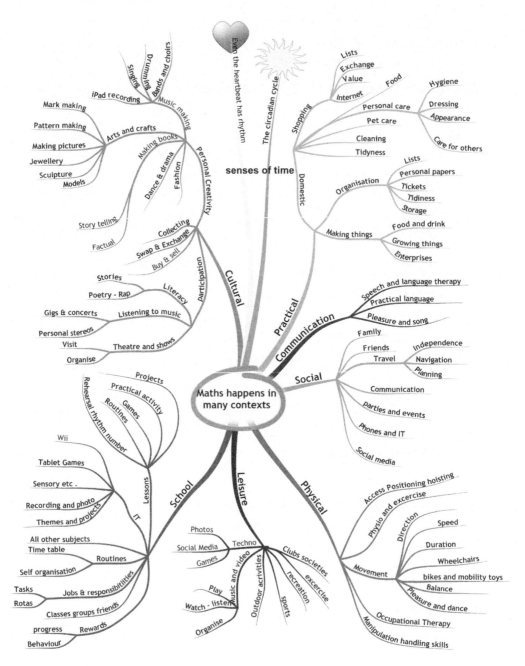

Figure 3.1 Maths occurs in many contexts

Life's maths

Mathematics is not only an abstract subject – it is a practical and social tool, with a huge root system of pre-numerate learning. Learning begins before birth and usually flourishes from sensory beginnings. Whatever curriculum model is adopted, those working with special children need to know how children usually develop mathematical ideas useful for living at a variety of levels. Such learning includes sensory and practical experiences that progress towards using problem solving, developing memory and growing degrees of abstract thought.

Schools are developing various curriculum models

It is becoming common for special schools to envisage layers of curriculum to accommodate the different needs of their pupils. For example, a model of three layers was developed in a collaboration between Castlewood School[1] and Penny Lacey, the revered and sadly missed special educationist whose work is referenced many times in this book. There is a similar approach at Fountaindale School. The layers underpin the formal learning described in a conventional curriculum, with descriptions that include sensory and concrete levels that work towards relevant learning and, for some pupils, adaptations of the conventional subjects.

 3.1 See online reading for more about schools developing various curriculum models

They often emphasise learning maths through cross-curricular approaches, such as taking exciting themes for the whole school to cover in creative ways (e.g. when the Olympic Games are on). On a visit to QE2 Jubilee School, I saw a great example of this using the topic of travel. The school entrance had a passport control booth and there were stacks of luggage. Classrooms had become environments from different continents – the outdoor play area was Venice. The whole school was a rich environment with lots of maths potential. The online reading for this chapter also describes a project at The Castle School in Cambridge, which shared a maths through literacy project with other local schools.

 3.2 Online reading – a maths through literacy project

Special aspects of a very special mathematics curriculum

Core learning

An appropriate curriculum for very special children will need to include levels of learning that the conventional curriculum takes for granted. Teachers need to understand where all learning begins – even the initial learning that children are usually born with, but that many special children either lack or don't use well. Perhaps we even need to help them grow such learning. This book will return to aspects of core knowledge and sensory development many times as we discuss how children build on their perceptions of the world – including the number sense, which precedes counting and is the basis of making comparisons.

Using the tools of learning

A section of this book describes how children use their senses, perception, manipulation, movement, attention and communication as 'tools of learning', and also outlines how difficulties with them are encountered by special children as they are learning to learn and think about life's maths. These are the tools of curious exploration, and children learn to use these tools by using them to learn.

Learning to learn

Learning to learn is a term that is also used in relation to theories about 'learning power', discussed by Guy Claxton (2002)[2] when talking about developing students' psychological 'dispositions towards learning', which include aspects of pupil engagement such as developing curiosity, persistence, collaborative skills, learning to use alternative strategies and developing confidence, all of which are also important for special learners. The ideas are not unrelated to the levels of engagement described in the Engagement Profile and Scale developed by the SSA Trust,[3] or the forms of engagement that the Rochford Review 2016 suggests are appropriate aspects of development to observe for children with complex needs.

Processes of learning

The processes through which children gather and make sense of information may include observation, imitation, play, communication, problem solving, instruction and more. While programmes of study for the typical curriculum (*at least beyond early years*) do not give much consideration to helping children master those kinds of processes, they are important in our special curriculum. This is because although they may be second nature to typically developing children, that is not the case for all special children. So a part of this book will outline the development of *processes of learning*, particularly as seen in different types of 'play', and some of the focus in those sections is on how adults interact with pupils to promote their *levels of engagement*, enabling them to:

- Become responsive

- Exercise curiosity

- Become interested in being discoverers

- Develop anticipation

- Initiate and persist in investigating problems

- Take problem solving on into new and wider situations

Developing thinking

Initially, this book may seem to be principally about the early levels of learning practical maths, but it is important to bear in mind that even doing practical things requires memory and forms of thinking. Mathematics and thinking are intertwined, so this book will start from fundamentals of thinking that are not included in the conventional maths curriculum – ideas such as object permanence and awareness of cause and effect. It will also progress through how children use 'practical action ideas' and move on towards more abstract thinking processes.

Developing counting and the 'big ideas'

Close to the end, the book will describe ideas and processes that underpin where the typical mathematics curriculum begins, *such as the perceptual process of subitising, which is not mentioned in the National Curriculum, but upon which understanding about counting depends.* Finally, the book will look at the sub-skills or 'parts of counting' and some of the 'big ideas' like comparisons and 'hierarchical inclusion' upon which the calculations of practical life and forms of abstract thinking depend.

 3.3 See online reading for a note relating how realistic mathematics education relates to this book

Notes

1 Castlewood School curriculum, www.castlewood.coventry.sch.uk/learning/curriculum
2 Claxton, G. (2002) *Building Learning Power: Helping Young People Become Better Learners.* TLO.
3 The Complex Learning Difficulties and Disabilities Research Project (2011) *Engagement Profile and Scale, SSAT, Wolverhampton,* www.complexneeds.org.uk/modules/Module-3.2-Engaging-in-learning---key-approaches/All/downloads/m10p040c/engagement_chart_scale_guidance.pdf

4 Sensory beginnings

Where does mathematical learning begin?

Many fundamental ideas of mathematics begin to develop earlier than words; they spring from the physical sensory experiences of space, movement, sequence, time, quantities, etc. There is a great deal of mathematical learning that usually takes place before children start school, by which time most have developed concepts that are the bedrock of 'thinking' and practical activities that support their later ability to use language, numbers, symbols and abstract ideas.

By continually exploring and refining play, children turn perceptions from their senses and memories of actions into 'sensory ideas'. These are ideas without words – I will refer to the way they use them as 'action thinking'. You can see action thoughts expressed in patterns of activity, like jumping and rolling, or in drawing – in fact, all physical actions are making memory ideas that go to every corner of practical life, thinking and maths. As these non-verbal ideas evolve, they make a web of practical 'schema'.[1] Later, they become connected to language and children can learn to express them in speech and communicate about them.

What important mathematicians have said

Iain Stewart said:

> The mathematical mind is rooted in the human visual, tactile and motor systems.

Einstein before him had written:

> My mathematical thinking initially involves visual and muscular processes.

What better people to testify for us that mathematics has sensory and practical beginnings, and a curriculum for mathematics or thinking needs to acknowledge stages before the use of words, numbers or symbols.

There are some mathematical senses

In a later chapter, we will discuss the parts that sensory systems play in our special curriculum because they are tools we use for learning. We will see that the way we use the range of sensory systems stretches much wider than the conventional idea of 'the five senses'. Appreciating the processes of sensory integration is vital for us, because we never use single senses, always combinations. We gather information together to create practical knowledge – which is mathematical in the widest sense. In fact, there are some areas of experience that we could even think of as 'mathematical senses'. They include:

- Sense of size

- Sense of quantity – which is exhibited in 'number sense'

- Senses of difference

- Senses of space – orientation, location and dimension

- Senses of movement – direction and speed

- Sense of rhythm and sequence

- Senses of time – interval -duration

- Senses of possession or loss

> **4.1 Online reading contains more thoughts about the mathematical senses**
>
> **4.2 Sensory integration and learning from sensory play**

Core knowledge

In the late 20th century, a great deal of research has illustrated that children are born with 'core knowledge' (Spelke & Kinzler, 2007),[2] which enables infants to organise their perceptions, giving them a means of starting to make sense of their environment through awareness of objects, persons, spatial relations and even 'numerosity'.

> Core knowledge, includes:
>
> - *Object representation* – infants are able to separate objects from the background.
>
> - *Awareness of people as agents of action* – they understand people can act and can change things.

- *Geometric spatial awareness* – they have awareness of orientation and interest in high-contrast environmental features such as edges.

- *Number sense* – infants are able to use perceptual memory to notice differences between groups.

  - Recent research in neuroscience also suggests that there are connections between our perceptions of time intervals and number sense (see online reading for chapter 25 on the sensory beginnings of number)

  Note: Though often described as 'number sense', at this stage it is a perceptual skill not initially connected to numerals or number systems. How these connections arise is one of the essences of this book.

Although core knowledge is the basis of all the rich cognitive skills that get us through life, it is usually ignored in typical curriculum development. Perhaps it is taken for granted because things like making sensory judgements for mobility, observing sizes or interacting with people are regarded as things that we do automatically – not a part of the 'subject'. But for our special pupils, these roots of learning are important.

The roots of a very special curriculum

The relationships between the roots of sensory experience and core knowledge – and the processes of exploration and problem solving through which practical mathematical ideas develop – are subtle and underestimated by the conventional academic curriculum. However, when children are affected by significant barriers to learning, we must take them into account.

A maths curriculum for very special children must:

- Begin at the sensory roots of learning

- Aim to help children learn to learn

- Help them appreciate their powers to cause and change things

- Include mathematical ideas that children usually develop before they start school

- Recognise the nature of their thinking processes

- Develop thinking that uses mathematical knowledge by engaging children in practical, social and cultural experiences

Learning to learn skills

Any curriculum for children that covers the early stages of 'thinking' or 'maths' needs to recognise that, as children build upon core knowledge, they are '*learning to learn'*. 'Learning to learn' skills are all those things that children naturally do to become active learners. They begin with using the *'tools for learning'* in *'processes of learning'* that evolve through exploration. Their tools are the senses and exploration skills that lead them to communications skills and learning to think.

They are skills that all pupils require

Learning to learn is clearly important for pupils with profound and multiple learning difficulties (PMLD) and many sources have documented them as important elements of a PMLD curriculum (Longhorn, 1993[3]; Routes for Learning[4]; Quest for Learning[5]). But developing learning fluency is important for all pupils. Sometimes it is good for learning to learn objectives to run in parallel with subject content objectives. Other times, they may be priorities in themselves, such as when a child has very disrupted attention that prevents them from participating in learning.

We all need to refine our learning to learn skills – even a skill like learning to count to three actually requires a range of sub-skills such as looking and touching objects, imitating speech sounds, etc., or advanced skills like learning the violin require finger exercises or joint attention to a teacher. So although the conventional curriculum takes them for granted – they are important.

 4.3 Online reading includes examples of learning to learn skills that underpin the ability to count three objects

The roots are part of the whole curriculum

The following diagram – the roots of maths (Fig. 4.1) – shows the whole curriculum: below the ground are the roots of mathematical learning and above are the various branches of the conventional curriculum.

The lower part shows mathematical learning that springs from roots of:

- Core knowledge that we are usually born with – but cannot take for granted with special children

- Tools for learning to learn – the physical and mental skills that children use to gather and integrate information

The branching roots extend to many finer skills; consequently, the root system is potentially enormous. For example:

- The 'theory of mind' branch could extend to include watching other people's actions, experiencing other people's responses, sharing things, giving, asking, etc.

- 'Boundaries' could include making boundaries, crossing boundaries, being inside, etc.

- 'Tracking' could include at different speeds, tracking objects, hand actions, lines, sounds, hiding and revealing, etc.

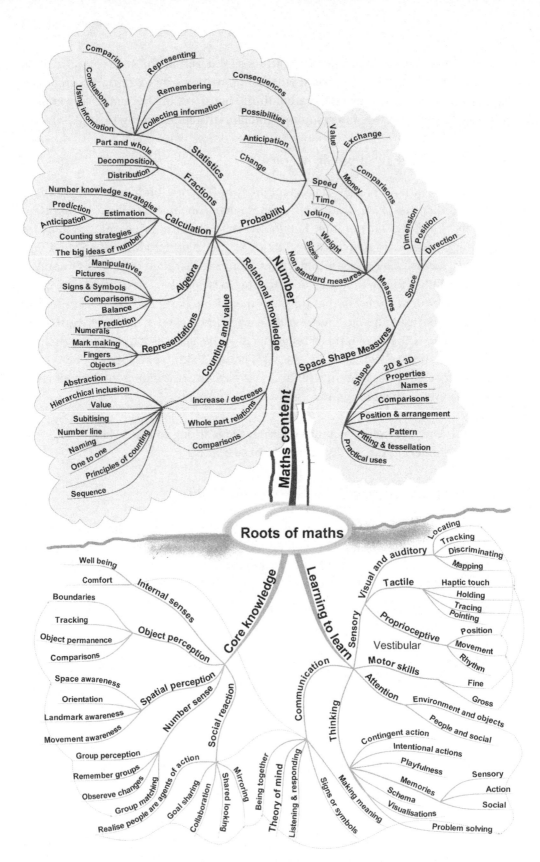

Figure 4.1 The roots of maths

The upper part shows aspects of learning within the strands of the conventional curriculum. Many of our special students do work on this part, but often at their own level of understanding and in ways that are relevant to their lives. For this reason, I have coined some of the labels in terms of learning that is relevant for them rather than the academic aspects of the mainstream programmes of study, for example including anticipation and prediction as elements of calculation.

Growing beyond sensory roots

Personal and social mathematics

Learning is driven by curiosity and ensuing exploration. There are two important aspects that typical children use, but that we may have to help our special children develop:

- Personal skills of exploration

- Social communication that enables them to share experiences

 4.4 See online reading for a fuller description of personal and social maths

Personal and social maths come together through communication

We only have to watch infants glancing back and forth between their playthings and adults to see the integration of their physical explorations and social interactions. They are clearly interested in cross-referencing and are aware that other people are helpful. In light of this, the integration of personal and social maths can be seen as being driven by a dynamic interest in communicating.

Where this is not the case – when children have very special needs – we have to recognise that teaching communication and learning interaction skills will be an important part of our special curriculum delivery. We need to learn how to lead children into communication and playfulness through the teaching arts of mirroring and modelling.

 4.5 See online reading about communicating to learn, introducing mirroring and modelling

Personal and social maths

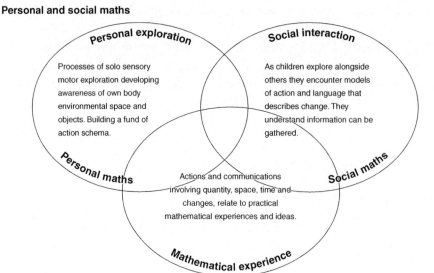

Personal exploration

Processes of solo sensory motor exploration developing awareness of own body environmental space and objects. Building a fund of action schema.

Social interaction

As children explore alongside others they encounter models of action and language that describes change. They understand information can be gathered.

Personal maths

Social maths

Actions and communications involving quantity, space, time and changes, relate to practical mathematical experiences and ideas.

Mathematical experience

Figure 4.2 Personal and social maths

Notes

1 Schema – children's thinking is in forms of thought that are grounded and expressed in actions and patterns of action.
2 Spelke, E. S. & Kinzler, K. D. (2007) Core knowledge. *Developmental Science* 10(1), 89–96.
3 Longhorn, F. (1993) *Prerequisites to learning for very special people.* Catalyst Education Resources Ltd.
4 Routes for Learning (2006) Welsh Assembly, http://learning.gov.wales/resources/browse-all/routes-for-learning-assessment-booklet/?lang=en
5 Quest for Learning, http://ccea.org.uk/curriculum/sen_inclusion/assessment/quest_learning

5 Introducing the parts of learning

Introducing tools and processes of learning

The tools children use for learning

Children use sensory and physical tools of enquiry to gather information from the environment. They include manipulation and motor skills and sensory, perceptual and attention skills. They all contribute to children's 'action thinking'. Usually, as childhood development progresses, these tools begin to include the communication skills that accelerate the social aspects of learning and thinking,

Sometimes our children have got particular tools missing or damaged. We need to understand how that affects them and find ways to compensate.

The processes children use to learn

The processes by which children use these tools are also the ways that they learn. The casual observer may call this 'play' without realising its importance. As children play, they choose, organise and use sensory information to do things. They cause effects and make things change, and as they remember their actions, *ideas* are formed. This is the everyday description of what psychologists describe as 'cognitive processes'.

Practical experience is mathematical content

The tools and processes I have described are not uniquely mathematical – they are used in practical life – but mathematical content is being covered when tools for learning are used in processes that relate to experiences and changes in quantity, such as size, value, sequence, space, shapes, etc.

If the tools are being used for responding to changes and solving practical problems, they are being used to think in a realm of mathematical activity.

Fig 5.1 shows that the parts of learning include three strands – tools, processes and content – that wind together.

The roots of learning mathematics in exploration and play

In this book, I am advocating that the processes of learning practical and mathematical thinking echo the same pathways as problem solving and play. As children follow a pathway from the earliest levels of developing playful attunement with carers through enjoying solitary sensory play and on through increasingly social levels of play towards cooperative learning, we can find appropriate ways of developing a wide range of practical and mathematical thinking – life maths – for very special pupils.

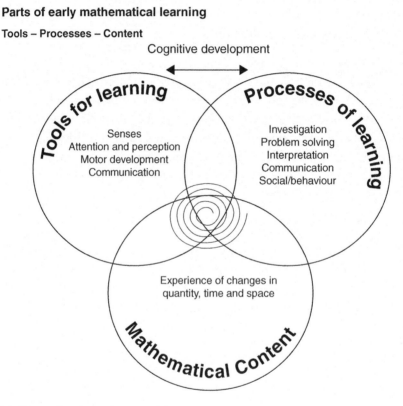

Parts of early mathematical learning

Tools – Processes – Content

Cognitive development

Tools for learning

Senses
Attention and perception
Motor development
Communication

Processes of learning

Investigation
Problem solving
Interpretation
Communication
Social/behaviour

Experience of changes in
quantity, time and space

Mathematical Content

Figure 5.1 Parts of early mathematical learning

Part 2
Tools for learning

6 Introducing the tools for learning

Learning to learn

The tools we have for learning to gather information in every aspect of life include:

- *Senses integrating together* – gathering information starts off the processes of learning.

- *Attention and perception* – to enable us to choose and make sense of stimulation.

- *Physical manipulation and mobility skills* – to enable us to gather and use information.

  - They help us repeat experiences and form memories of sensory experiences and physical actions that are our first forms of 'thinking'.

- *Social and behaviour skills* – to enable social orientation towards involvement with others in learning.

- *Communication skills* – to enable us to seek more and share information from other people. These are how we extend our action into mental thought.

Typical children usually use all these tools with ease, but there are many ways that our special children have difficulties. They often need support in learning to use them – in effect, they often need to learn how to learn.

Learning to learn develops through real experiences

In learning cycles, as children are driven by curiosity, they use their tools to gather information, but practice also improves their ability to use these tools. So, it is always important to emphasise that motivating physical and sensory practice is an important part of our curriculum. But that is not to advocate teaching skills through isolated rehearsal or having a narrow view of curriculum content that is structured by developmental checklists. The skills that children learn must connect to real-life situations, and the way we teach skills should encourage children to connect them to *thinking* about practical actions. A feature of our teaching should be modelling and providing commentary describing what's happening and what could happen, all the time connecting the child's actions to new possibilities.

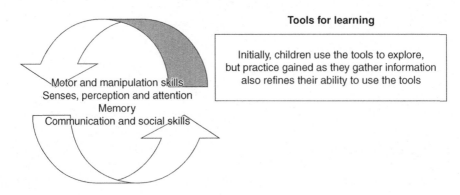

Tools for learning

Initially, children use the tools to explore, but practice gained as they gather information also refines their ability to use the tools

Motor and manipulation skills
Senses, perception and attention
Memory
Communication and social skills

Figure 6.1 Tools for learning

About the tools and mathematical learning

Without specific teaching, children usually build up vast experience of people and practical understanding of life. The development of real-world mathematical thinking is bound up with this knowledge. For example, they have innate ideas about common objects and space and through them are able to anticipate or judge actions and changes.

When children have all their sensory facilities, they are usually able to learn a great deal from imitating other people. They observe and hear what people say and do in everyday contexts and become able to memorise, visualise, physically replicate, express and think about objects and the effects of changes. These processes are mathematical life learning in action.

When there are difficulties with the tools

Motor and manipulation

When children have difficulties handling things or moving around, the independent exploration of shape, form, weight, sequence, etc., that is needed to form action ideas is inhibited. We need to find ways to adapt experiences and motivate participation.

Even pupils with moderate difficulties, such as those whose eye and hand movements are clumsy, can find that motor control takes so much effort that concentration and the flow of learning is lost. The knock-on effects of poor motor abilities is enormous, as is evidenced in conditions like dyspraxia (Dyspraxia Foundation, 2016).[1]

Senses and perception

Some sensory limitations are clearly evident to the observer, such as a blind person's limited mobility, but others may be less so. For example, hearing loss has often led to even typically developing children being categorised as slow until the condition was diagnosed. Hidden senses like our sense of body position, proprioception or pressure have inestimable influence on our ideas of space, etc.

Sometimes, sensory difficulties occur through neurological causes rather than physical difficulties with sense organs, and in these cases, it is often very difficult for the casual observer to perceive the cause of the child's problems. There are issues like dyslexia or aphasia, which sometimes go undetected in the population of typical children. I would suggest that many pupils with SLD or autism may suffer their effects, but their presence is hidden under the children's general 'diagnosis'. In consequence, useful approaches to specific teaching strategies could be missed. *The perceptual problems that cause dyscalculia are a case in point that will be addressed in later chapters.*

We may describe senses separately, but in life we always use them together in integrated ways, and sensory integration activities are our way into finding alternative strategies for living and learning.

Attention difficulties

These can disrupt children's ability to follow threads of exploration and draw information from communication. Autism is widely regarded as an attention 'problem', particularly when it is defined by the triad of behaviours that often constitute its diagnosis:

1. Social behaviour

2. Language impairment

3. Rigid, stereotyped behaviour

The triad tends to focus on symptoms rather than causes, whereas it may be useful to focus on the sensory causes of the behaviour and strive to find ways to communicate and arrange resources and environments that enable pupils to learn.

Memory

Poor short-term memory reduces children's abilities to follow and repeat sequential activity or to move from concrete to abstract thought by recalling representations. It is important to regard the development of visualisation and memory as part of teaching the root skills of thinking and mathematics. I will return to this in chapters on mathematical thinking

Communication

Problems with the nuances of language sequences, such as expressing reactions or handling questions, make it more difficult for special children to absorb ideas.

Typical children understand that language can be used for sharing and as a form of enquiry. They habitually express curiosity and are used to raising questions in their talk. It often seems that children with SLD are not so aware of the how to raise problems. Indeed, it often seems that children simply don't understand that they don't understand. This is compounded because, as we will see later, adults have a tendency to use fewer questions and more closed or directive speech with special children. In the chapters to come on developing play, I spend some time discussing ways of modelling language and provoking problem solving.

Some examples of special children and using tools for learning

There are many ways in which difficulties with the tools for learning can affect children, all of which are complex. Three examples are summarised below.

 6.1 Online reading includes a fuller descriptions of the examples

Janine

Janine has such complex physical and sensory difficulties that it is impossible for us to imagine how she perceives the world and objects in it. The example describes ways of working on her body map and spatial mapping.

Clyde

Clyde is a child with Down syndrome who has finger manipulation difficulties that both hinder the physical organisation of objects and overloads mental processes, making the use of memory difficult. The example includes using games like 'greedy granny' or 'hungry hippo' to provide motivating contexts for practising parts of counting.

Jack

Jack's autism makes it difficult for him to learn from others by sharing focus on relevant aspects of stimuli. Though his optical vision is fine, how he uses it is disrupted by perceptual/neurological difficulties, so the sense he makes of his environment is different. The example relates to finding ways to help him share 'looking' with others.

Note

1 Dyspraxia Foundation (2016), https://dyspraxiafoundation.org.uk/dyspraxia-adults/

7 Physical skills at the beginning of thinking

The beginning of exploration is the beginning of thinking

All early years theorists have outlined ways that children develop through movements towards thinking, and this chapter draws on the common ground between some of them.

Fine motor manipulation

In the typical development of children's dexterity, we observe the hands as organs of performance that facilitate practical life. But beyond physical manipulation, they are also organs of senses and perception that gather information through touch and movement. These roles will be discussed in the coming chapters, as will the more surprising roles they have in processes of thinking and representing thoughts and number. So, when we speak of fine motor skills we are exploring much more than manipulation dexterity. But SLD or PLD children often lack fluency or sometimes even have profoundly disabling difficulties with the hands, so our teaching needs to compensate or extend their range of sensory exploration by supporting tactile experience – developing finger and hand manipulations – and integrating reaching and grasping movements and haptic touch (i.e. the touch we use to recognise the shape of objects and control pressure). It involves our experience of stroking and grasping, the shapes we make with our fingers or actions and the pressures we feel. Experiences such as hand massage may be much more important than the casual bystander may think. The hand is not only driven by the brain – it also informs it.

 7.1 Online reading includes a note on hand massage

Finding out – heuristic play

The work of Elinor Goldschmeid in the 1980s described how manipulative skills are part of refining thinking. She coined the phrase 'heuristic play' for infants' self-directed play. Her work has been continued by Anita Hughes (2016).[1] Goldschmeid is best remembered for the idea of the 'treasure baskets', allowing infants to select, examine and use objects in any way they like. She observed that the time they spent handling and mouthing objects "is a time of finding out what the object is like," whilst later, as handling skills develop, they move on to ask "What can I do with it?" by investigating possibilities like banging, placing, rolling, dumping, filling, stacking, fitting inside each other, balancing, etc. The imagination stage when the child thinks about "What can this *be*?" comes later.

The sensory curriculum ideas of Flo Longhorn set out in her classic book, *A Sensory Curriculum for Very Special People* (1988),[2] set the scene for teachers of very special children, and her maths book, *Numeracy for Very Special People* (2000),[3] contains a myriad of ideas about manipulation skills that have inspired a new generation of teachers in very special schools.

Direct patterning

Geoffrey Waldon (1980),[4] who worked extensively with learning-disabled children, observed that many special children don't engage in such self-motivated play and so fail to begin to develop the patterns of exploratory action that are necessary for cognitive development.[5] The patterns of actions he observed included banging, placing, piling, pairing, matching, separating and sequencing, and they are included (with others) in Fig. 7.1. In contrast to learning through free movement, Waldon advocated adults directly patterning children's actions, and situations often arise when adults might feel it seems necessary to guide manipulation (e.g. when teaching feeding or letter formation teaching). Approaches that use physical direction require sensitive consideration, and some practitioners, such as Veronica Sherborne, whose ideas about movement I will discuss shortly, have different viewpoints.

 7.2 See online reading for more about Waldon's patterns of action and functional learning as well as a note on direct patterning. There is more discussion on working with the hands in Chapters 12 and 19.

Sharing looking and exploration – learning together

Working alongside children to extend their use of fine motor skills entails modelling actions and language whilst participating together, sharing the purposes and the pleasure of handling and attending to objects. Working in this socially interactive way is a major theme of this book.

Different children will need different kinds of help; for example:

■ Some will need to learn to share attention to stimuli – reacting to sensory experiences together.

■ Others need to develop fluency or coordination in the physical skills of reaching, handling, taking and giving, all of which enable them to share.

■ Others need to appreciate and learn how to share responses and cause and effect.

There are other examples and different priorities for different children, but they are all aspects of learning to learn and as such are essential roots of a maths curriculum. The spirit of Goldschmeid's ideas, and those of Lilli Nielsen and Flo Longhorn, can be seen in the work of many present-day special practitioners as they set up sensory learning environs for PMLD children and students.

Some of the fine motor activities that we can work into our shared activities
Early years pioneers like Froebel, Montessori and Waldon have all stressed the importance of children learning to organise movement and handling things. Fig. 7.1 includes activities through which children develop ideas that could be included in practical and sensory sessions at different levels, and the text box that follows gives examples that are expanded in the online reading.

7.3 Online reading includes examples of fine motor play that provide fundamental mathematical experience

Figure 7.1 Fine motor experiences

Some examples where activities including fine motor skills might provide contexts for mathematical experience.

The examples overlap with many learning areas:

- Sensory trays, treasure baskets, memory boxes/bags

- Shared hand and finger massage

- Clapping and banging

- Play with small toys

- Sorting – separating and matching

- Placing things

- Connecting

- Nesting and stacking (e.g. cups, storage boxes, chairs and bricks) illustrate the concept of 'hierarchical inclusion'

- Handling cards and pictures

- iPad or tablet: wide range of games developing finger manipulation and looking

Gross motor activity

Movement and our sense of space

Movement is a primary means by which we experience space, direction, speed, time, weight and force. Our understanding of sequences and rhythm originates from core knowledge and develops through moving.

In later chapters, we will see that the origins of early mathematical ideas (including counting) have roots in our spatial awareness and depend on visualisation. However, many SLD children and children with neurological disorders such as such as dyspraxia[6] have difficulties with movement, and many PMLD children have no experience of independent mobility. So, developing the ease and experience of fluent body movement and kinaesthetic memory through experiences such as those depicted in Fig. 7.2 is important for their development.

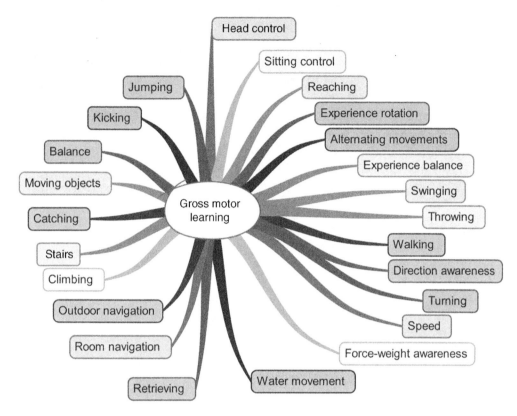

Figure 7.2 Gross motor skills

Fig. 7.2 illustrates some of the aspects of mobility experiences we need to arrange for children to either experience or do. They all need to be illustrated and emphasised by a rich commentary.

The work of Lilli Nielsen (1992)[7] developing the 'little room' and 'resonance boards' introduced us to ideas (that predated today's baby gyms) about devising learning environments immediately around children in which they can scan and reach independently to find stimulation and create deliberate actions. We often find sensory corners and tents in today's special classrooms. The Hirstwood Training website and YouTube channel are fantastic sources of high- *and* low-tech ideas from Richard the human dynamo (Hirstwood, 2016).[8]

 7.4 Online reading example of a mini-sensory room improvised in a cardboard box

Veronica Sherborne (2001)[9] stressed that movement plays a crucial role in the development of all children. Her practices of sharing by '*feeding in movement*' have been used extensively with special needs children and adults, including those with very limited movement and those on the autistic spectrum.

Moving together can be a beautiful thing. Sherborne describes two basic object-ives of Sherborne movement as 'awareness of self' and 'awareness of others'. I have no hesitation in saying that the mapping body image through intrinsic sharing of space, movement and rhythm also makes an important contribution to mathemat-ical life knowledge.

The following text box includes just some suggestions of activities that are good for motivating life maths, both because they involve practicing social and phys-ical skills and because they provide opportunities for including mathematical experiences like counting, scoring, timing, gaining or losing.

Some examples of gross motor activities that contribute to mathematical learning.

- Games including sequential moving/stepping/jumping

- Directional reaching and placing

- Throwing, casting and retrieving

- Balance challenges or Twister games

- Obstacle courses or trim trails

- Rough and tumble

- Balloon keepy-uppy

- Swimming or hydro games

- Rebound therapy

- Nintendo Wii

- All forms of practical tasks

 7.5 Online reading provides more examples of gross motor activities

Notes

1 Hughes, A. M. (2016) *Developing Play for the Under 3s. The Treasure Basket and Heuristic Play. Third edition.* Oxford: Routledge.
2 Longhorn, F. (1988) *A Sensory Curriculum for Very Special People.* London: Souvenir Press.
3 Longhorn, F. (2000) *Numeracy for Very Special People.* Catalyst Education Resources.
4 Waldon, G. (1980) revised (1985) *Understanding Understanding: An Introduction to a Personal View of the Educational Needs of Children,* www.waldonassociation.org.uk/pdfs/library-index/waldon-associates-understanding-understanding.pdf

5 Waldon uses the term 'learning how to learn tools' to describe these activities, whereas elsewhere in this book I often use the term 'learning to learn tools' in a different sense – to refer to our senses, attention and perceptual skills.

6 Dyspraxia Foundation (2016), http://dyspraxiafoundation.org.uk/about-dyspraxia/

7 Nielsen, L. (1992) *Space and Self.* Copenhagen: Sikon Press.

8 Hirstwood, R. (2016) Video of using electroluminescent wire in a special education setting, www.youtube.com/watch?v=lZI29o7hx-k

9 Sherborne, V. (2001) *Developmental Movement for Children. 2nd edition.* Worth Publishing, www.sherbornemovementuk.org/sherborne-developmental-movement.html

8 Schema – first patterns of thinking

Starting from the reflexes they have at birth, typical infants remember their physical actions and the results. If they were useful or pleasurable they repeat them, and if they need to they refine them. This process continues with all actions and imitations, and they particularly practice them in their heuristic, 'free-flow play' (Siraj-Blatchford & Brock 2016).[1] It is not entirely random – as it progresses, they both use and develop patterns of actions that psychologists describe as 'schema'. You can see children repeat actions to test them and apply them to new settings. Long before they connect them to related verbal language, they are 'action ideas' – they remember and reuse them. In effect, they are thoughts that are used before children have words; in fact, later mental thoughts develop from them. So physical playing, refining and remembering actions are really important in learning, and the way that all the sensory and perceptual learning is gradually refined into patterns of action is a fascinating and crucial element of our story.

Major schema

Early years practitioners have illustrated that the patterns of action stem from just a small number of reflex actions and ideas that interest the infants. Chris Athey (2007)[2] observed four major schema:

- Vertical and horizontal movements

- Circular movements

- Enveloping or containing

- Going through or crossing boundaries

But these develop into a wider range of manipulation and movement schema that children apply and explore in their play and practical activities. It is the useful application of these actions that transforms sensory play into knowledge.

Schema and mathematical thinking

Some examples of schema that develop from the four major ones are:

- *Connecting* – joining and putting together, experiencing progressive increase

- *Enclosing and enveloping* – which are different ways of being interested in 'insideness'

- *Posting* – through letter boxes and tubes is a root of one to one sequencing

- *Dabbing* – initial haphazard mark making develops into more ordered activity at the root of mathematical mark making

- *Orientation* – exploring body orientation leads to wider understandings about position

- *Moving and transporting* – children may move objects or collections of objects from one place to another, experiencing progressive changes of quantity, conservation, space, direction and position, and the language of position and change

These are just some examples because the range of schema develops infinitely as they interrelate and evolve from each other. One of the ways that children usually translate actions into mental representations is through their playful mark making and drawing, which rehearses many patterns of action. 'Mark Making Matters' (2008)[3] is an excellent publication with a section about development of children's mathematical mark making. There is a table of schema in the online reading.

 8.1 Online reading – some schema that contribute to mathematical thinking

Schema are in all our actions

Since schema are constituent parts of all practical activity, we can support exploration through the infinite range of life skills and games related to the roots of maths. Sometimes children are particularly interested in one form of schema, sometimes they will show several – and combine them into useful actions. They are applicable in different ways at various ages and ability levels. Patterns occur right across the range from sensory motor to abstract thinking. Children often explore particular schema then move on, but later revisit to explore with greater maturity of action and language.

Schema work at different levels of development

Though schema begin with reflex and physical skills, their level of expression changes as children's levels of learning mature. I have added a first 'reflex level' to the four overlapping levels that Tina Bruce (1987)[4] outlined:

1. *Reflex level* – children gain control of reflex actions to perform useful and enjoyable movement. This may happen with natural ease for most children. Many children with very special needs have great difficulties, and these need to be a focus of maths at a sensory level.

2. *Sensorimotor level* – children use their senses and physical action to explore and change things.

3. *Symbolic level* – beginning to exercise imaginative thought, children begin to use object to represent something else (e.g. they may push a Lego brick around as a play car or use a box as a doll's bed).

4. *Functional dependency level* – incorporates knowledge of cause and effect into their play, reflecting awareness about causes and consequences (e.g. they may pretend their 'car' has stopped because it needs petrol or that when there are already two in a bed there is no more room for another baby).

5. *Abstract thought level* – able to reason verbally about the significance of actions.

Whilst it is possible that a mixed-ability special classroom could include pupils across at least the first four of these levels, the majority of our special pupils will be at the earlier levels, perhaps practising sensorimotor skills or beginning to attribute some representational meaning to objects or toys. Our roles are to introduce practical application of skills or promote their thinking about both cause and effect and symbolic representations. Modelling language of quantity, number, change, space, shape, etc., as we play with children is our important contribution to moving them towards abstract thoughts.

Schema are revisited as children's abilities mature

Children revisit and reuse schema at different levels as their abilities mature. They apply different levels of thinking. For example, a very sensory player may explore circularity with arm or limb movements, a concrete player may draw circles or push toys round circular tracks, whilst an abstract player may attribute meanings to the circles they draw, saying they represent things.

Sensory play is the beginning of thinking and, in many ways, it continues, and all of the forms of schema overlap for everybody – even adults use physical schema.

 8.2 Online reading includes a diagram that illustrates levels of progression from sensory to abstract thinking

Schema can help our observation and planning

Understanding how schema contribute to the development of children's 'thinking' helps us see progress and manage learning opportunities, particularly where children become obsessive or stuck in certain patterns that create difficult behaviour such as throwing or banging. Understanding the progression of schema can help us think where behaviour has come from, what its original value *was* and look for ways of using it to move on.

For example: since two of the values of the banging phase are to develop tool use and sequential rhythm, perhaps we can participate with our enthusiastic banger by banging alternate drums or using sticks to make rhythm, in this way we might shift his interest to more varied – and useful – sequential actions such as learning to control speed and force or learning to coordinate speech and action. Or we might seek to interest a child who throws things in a game aiming at targets with a suspended ball.

Awareness of schema is a useful lens for both seeing progress and planning

The following example illustrates how observing Jed's mark making can prime our planning and provide us with thoughts about his progress if we observe that Jed is progressing from random scribble towards making horizontal lines.

We might plan

- To improve his ideas and control of horizontal movement. In addition to his mark making, we could involve Jed in thinking about exercising some linear control in other contexts (e.g. playing a game of making lines along a track with a model car that has paint on its wheels or cutting straight lines in dough with a roller cutter to make finger biscuits).

Or we might observe progress

- By noting how well he engages in applying his horizontal actions in different contexts.

- Observing how well Jed responds in these learning contexts is important.

- Current suggestions proposed by the Rochford Review (2016)[5] about describing his levels of engagement in a lesson activity using the engagement profile developed by the Complex Learning Difficulties and Disabilities [CLDD] research project[6]) would give us a useful perspective about the quality of the lessons for him.

- But to show the full story, we need to know not only *how well* he is engaged, but also *what he is engaging in*. This includes the content in the context.

- We also need to reflect on how his actions and thinking are developing. Awareness of how children learn through schema provides a good framework of knowledge the teacher can use for observation and description.

A good picture of progress requires:

- *Observation of levels of engagement* – the extent to which they are able to engage in learning activities

- *Describing the content* – what the child is experiencing

- *Comment on levels of action* – the nature of their physical actions and how schema are maturing

- *Comment on levels of thinking* – from pre-intentional action (via concrete thinking, etc.) to social and abstract thinking

Notes

1 Siraj-Blatchford, J. & Brock, L. (2016) *Putting the Schema Back Into Schema Theory and Practice: An Introduction to Schema Play.* Poole: Schema Play Publications. This recent publication by Siraj-Blatchford and Brock provides references for those readers who are interested in how schema relate to typically developing children.
2 Athey, C. (1990) *Extending Thought in Young Children: A Parent–Teacher Partnership.* London: Paul Chapman.
3 Mark Making Matters (2008) National Strategies – Early Years, www.foundationyears.org. uk/wp-content/uploads/2011/10/Mark_Marking_Matters.pdf
4 Bruce, T. (1987) *Early Childhood Education.* London: Hodder and Stoughton.
5 Rochford Review (2017) Primary school pupil assessment: Rochford Review recommendations, www.gov.uk/government/uploads/system/uploads/attachment_data/file/644729/Rochford_consultation_response.pdf
6 CLDD Engagement Profile and Scale. The Complex learning difficulties and disabilities research project, http://complexneeds.org.uk/modules/Module-3.2-Engaging-in-learning---key-approaches/All/downloads/m10p040c/engagement_chart_scale_guidance.pdf

9 Introducing the senses

The senses

Because the 'distance' senses of sight and hearing reach out and collect so much information at our conscious level, we regard them as primary and cannot imagine life without them. Yet whilst many blind people manage good mobility, can you imagine how it would be if you could not sense the position of your body in space? What would it be like if you were unable to control the movement of your limbs to walk, or your hand to reach out? There are two little-mentioned sensory systems that work together and enable us to understand and control our position, movement and forces – they are proprioception (a sense of body and limb position) and the vestibular sense (sometimes described as an equilibrium sense); we would quite literally be lost in space without them.

So the common phrase of 'the five senses' is an underestimation. I have just suggested another two sensory systems, and as we go on, more will become apparent. There are aspects of sensing that don't get conscious credit and a web of interactions between our senses[1] that generate the flow of life we perceive.

A philosophical thought

Where does our awareness of geometry begin?

- The vestibular system senses circular and angular momentum and linear acceleration. It uses our sense of gravity in order to monitor the orientation of our body. Without that and other sensory information, we would not understand the arrangement of our environment. So you might ask yourself – where does understanding of geometry begin?

The sense of position deriving from gravitational pull influences us even before we are born and must be instrumental to developing understanding of the space around us.

Sensory integration

No sense works in isolation. In an example in the online reading for Chapter 6, I noted that for Jack that "the eye looks but the brain sees." Shortly we will see that the vestibular sense actually has direct interconnections with the eye.[2] This means that even the simple act of standing uses our experiences of sight, touch and physical movement all together.

 9.1 Online reading includes an illustration of sensory integration in action.

Typical children constantly develop sensory integration as they are engaged in physical activity. They develop neural pathways and a fund of subconscious knowledge that can be called on for conscious or subconscious actions that very often occur alongside adult commentary as they are engaged in 'serve and return' communications together.

 9.2 Online reading includes reference to how 'serve and return' interactions build brain architecture.

When there are sensory difficulties

There are many ways that sensory problems affect learning, not only easily observable sensory impairments such as vision or hearing, but also more hidden conditions. There is a range of neurological learning difficulties that are sometimes dubbed 'sensory processing disorders' or related to attention or perceptual deficits, whose symptoms and causes overlap. Autism, attention deficit hyperactivity disorder (ADHD), dyspraxia, dyslexia and dyscalculia are all examples of conditions where disrupted sensory input can cause the child extreme disorientation. Some children are labelled difficult when they react to disruptive input by developing habits or unaccountable behaviours that get in the way of learning. Readers will find a fund of very accessible knowledge on Becky Lyndon's Sensory Spectacle website[3] and YouTube channel.[4]

External and internal senses
We gather information from external senses – '*exteroception*'. Most teachers are aware of their importance, but less is written about the effects on learning of '*interoception*' (spdlife.org),[5] which involves the senses of internal organ function. They detect responses for the regulation of our body, such as hunger, thirst, respiration, heart rate, digestion, pain, etc. They may also make contributions to fundamental learning; for example, is it possible that the child's sense of hunger along with the circadian cycle is related to developing understand of the passage of time

in the pattern of a day; or the feeling of satiation after feeding may be attached to language ideas and about 'enough' imparted through communication with caregivers. There will be mention later about how the sense of gravitational pull may be a component of the core knowledge and how proprioception contributes to spatial understanding.

Not usually listed in education diagnoses of special needs are the internal senses, particularly pain, which may actually have powerful effects that can disturb learning, particularly through affecting attention (e.g. creating anxieties or unusual urges or desires, such as keeping moving to maintaining the excitement of the heartbeat, or eating disorders).

Nadia's learning demeanour

Nadia has profound disabilities and she does not speak. She used to avoid interactions, and our attempts to engage her in sensory-sharing play usually led to her rejecting the sensory toys and turning away. Her stomach was sometimes bloated and we did notice that at those times she was particularly negative regarding both social interaction and feeding.

After a blood test, she was diagnosed with coeliac disease and her diet was changed. Gradually, Nadia became more sociable and seemed to anticipate sensory interaction sessions with pleasure. She moved from rejection towards a sunnier disposition and developed an inclination towards social interactions and curiosity. Our theory is that her digestive system had been a continual cause of pain, which she could not tell us about and dominated her attention.

In each of the next few chapters, I will discuss working with particular sensory systems. This is for convenience – it is a way of trying to keep some clarity because in reality they all overlap and interact. As you read, you will see that emphasis always eventually falls on the importance that sensory integration has in providing alternative and compensatory experiences due to the senses working together.

Finally, I must mention that whilst these chapters often seem to focus on the convention of seven sensory systems, you can be sure there will be other senses like gravity or rhythm making their presence felt – and not least will be 'number sense' – but that is for a future chapter.

Notes

1 You may be able to reel of a list of senses or sub-senses like a sense of time, sense of size and sense of rhythm, and later we will even discuss 'number sense'.

2 The vestibule-ocular reflex stimulates eye movement in the opposite direction to head movement and keeps an image on the centre of the visual field.

3 Lyddon, B. (2017) Sensory Spectacle, www.sensoryspectacle.co.uk

4 Lyddon, B. (2017) Sensory Spectacle YouTube page, www.youtube.com/results?search_query=sensory+spectacle

5 Spdlife.org. Interoception – the sense of internal organ function, http://spdlife.org/aboutspd/senses/interoception.html

10 About vision

The range of visual impairment

Across the population of children that I am writing about, there is a wide range of levels of visual impairment. Some children, particularly those with Down syndrome, will have problems that are correctable by glasses, without which their learning may be affected as they may miss detail. It is too often the case that such children are blithely unaware of what they are missing, and it is important for us to be vigilant, both managing their glasses and being aware of possible problems e.g. when recognising symbols or discerning groups (Porter, 2016).[1]

There will be some pupils with more profound disabilities whose perceptions are very significantly disrupted by eye conditions that reduce or distort sight (e.g. focus or field of vision). Still others have multi-sensory impairment and consequently experience the world in a very different way to most of us. It take leaps of imagination to appreciate what their perceptions are like, and in this book there is only space for an overview of approaches to teaching them.

 10.1 See online reading for more information about 'objects of reference' and 'sounds of intent' and a link to the **Royal National Institute for the Blind (RNIB)** website.

Learning from social observation

Typically, children learn a lot by watching people in practical activities or watching peers play – associating actions and speech to form ideas. But social and play environments are often fast moving and fluid, so when visual impairment limits scanning, it inhibits responses and imitations, disrupting play and practical learning. We have to find ways to support our special children's access to experience of life and play, and that includes aspects of life maths.

Visual memory of the environment

Most of us are able to use visual memories of the places we are in. We can construct both short- and longer-term memory maps. For most children, particular visual experiences recur so often that they are able to construct and retain generalised 'visualisations' about things and groups (e.g. we have mental ideas about what 'twoness' or 'threeness' is, or ideas about size and shapes) and we use such mental imagery as tools of anticipation and thinking. But children with visual difficulties will not have the same visual memory maps, and we need to support them using tactile and kinaesthetic memory patterns to create versions of 'visualisation' utilising other senses.

Working with visual impairment

Alternative sensory stimuli

When working with visually impaired children who need alternative sensory information to build memory maps and ideas, we need to be aware of using audible and tactile clues to give contextual clues (e.g. volume or direction of sound may help their spatial perceptions); touch clues or exaggerated movement gestures, or tapping or scraping objects, all contribute to multisensory 'looking'. They can provide orientation to help tracking sequential objects to develop spatial awareness, or memory of groups or quantities and perceptions of changes. Remember, even for typically developing children, clapping, stepping, jumping, making gestures, etc., are all staples of traditional games through which they learn about things like sequential order or increase/decrease, and through which they develop skills and memory tags, all of which we need to harness to compensate for visual impairment.

Jerome

My friend who is registered blind and is highly intelligent and amusing has a vocal click he makes with the back of his palate. The echo tells him something about the size of the place he is in, because the sound in his head is different in a washroom or a cathedral – he calls it his Batman navigation system. He is using another sense to find out about space, just as using touching, making gestures or nodding our head as we count is part of tracking counting.

Guiding thinking through commentary

The use of adult commentary to guide children's exploration and thinking is a recurring theme in this book. There are three roles that can be used:

- *Commentary* – describing the sequence of events as they happen

■ *Connecting* – pointing out connections to other experiences or things

■ *Creating* – making opportunities by prompting reactions and promoting new choices

RNIB online guidance[2] discusses ways of supporting blind children by maintaining commentary that describes structure and points out links and opportunities.

 10.2 Online reading includes links to these RNIB resources on social inclusion

---

A few ideas about vision and resources

It is useful to think of resources that will attract attention.

■ Use counting objects that have resonance, or shakers.

■ Many everyday objects have strong sensory properties (e.g. pan scrubs or brushes).

■ Use toys that encourage tracking and location, including light and sound toys.

■ Let them familiarise themselves with objects and environs before activities start.

■ Use visual resources that have contrasts and boundaries.

■ Use narrow-beam spotlit work areas or torches used as pointers.

■ Use ultraviolet resources and torches.

■ Use work areas in corners, tents or using work boxes.

■ Use iPad apps for looking, touching and tracing (*search for Ian Bean or Understood.com*).

Conversely, think about limiting visual confusion in the environment.

■ Avoid glare over reflective surfaces.

■ Avoid patterned backgrounds, floors or furnishings.

■ Use dark backgrounds to provide clear contrast.

■ Sensory rooms with too much going on can be disorientating.

 10.3 Online reading provides some more ideas about vision and resources

Pupils with profound disabilities

With PMLD children, our role may be to start children's exploration processes and motivate them to learn to look and share looking. There is much excellent work done in sensory rooms encouraging attention to stimulus by focusing on points of interest and tracking, and there are also many visual stimulation apps for tablet screens. But the experience of manipulating real things remains of primary importance and both 'Vision for Doing'[3] (Aitken & Buultjens, 1992)[4] and Focus on Foundation (RNIB, 2011)[5] are still good sources of advice[6] on this. Both of these stress types of stimulation that activate the child rather than allowing them to remain passive, and both emphasise the importance of everyday items and toys and developing active use of touch (see later discussions in the section on touch).

Working at different levels

Exploration in 'face space'

Some PLD pupils may need us to work in their 'face space', sharing facial communication and developing eye movement and tracking (McLinden & McCall, 2002),[7] or introducing tactile experience with hands and objects near to *or on* the face in order to relate vision and touch to exploration of objects.

Exploration in body space

As children develop as 'responders', we should develop their body map and awareness of limb position, reaching into the wider environment. Connect their visual awareness and proprioception to deliberate cause and effect.

Extending into social space

As children become motivated 'participators', enabling them to participate in parallel play and practical experiences is our priority. Stroking a child's arm may not seem much to you, but if that child has no/little movement *and* poor vision, how else can they build their body map and spatial perception than through other people's touch

Neural visual difficulties

Some children experience problems with vision that stem from neural rather than optical difficulties – though their eyes work, their brain processing is disrupted. There are suggestions that causes relate to light wavelength sensitivity (Meares, 1980),[8] and interferences may be triggered by factors like brightness, colour or contrast that disturb the integration of visual timing with the other senses. A range of conditions are associated with such perceptual stresses, including dyslexia, synaesthesia, autism and ADHD. Though not without controversy, there is increasing interest in the use of tinted lenses as described by Helen Irlen (1999)[9] for reducing these effects, particularly on text. Sensory distortions in autism are also discussed by Phoebe Caldwell.[10]

Perceptual difficulties may be difficult to pin down

We all have individual 'ways of seeing', and these will include a unique set of visual tolerances; for example, tolerance for the strain of night driving, flashing lights or even bright sunlight varies from person to person. Perceptual difficulties are difficult to identify. It is quite possible that unless they are pronounced, some people may live with perceptual difficulties they are unaware of. Many children may have mild or undiagnosed difficulties.

A wide range of effects are caused by this disruption of sensory integration, and because they can be caused by either oversensitivity (hyper) or undersensitivity (hypo), they are sometimes paradoxical.

They cause many problems at different levels, such as distortions that could make reading difficult through to disruptions that can make environments frightening – and learning *impossible* – unless they are dealt with.

 10.4 Online reading describes some neural visual difficulties children may experience. This is also covered in more depth in Chapter 13 and Online Reading 13.2

Any of the effects would understandably be causes of confusion and the avoidant behaviours that are common with autism spectrum disorder pupils, such as looking away, using short glances or 'stimming' – stereotypic behaviour, often near the eyes, such as hand-flapping and finger-flicking, which are distressed or aggressive responses in difficult lighting.[11] Our first challenge is to help pupils affected by visual disruption develop learning to learn skills, particularly sharing attention and looking. They need environments that minimise perceptual stress from glare, visual clutter, etc., and communication strategies akin to intensive inter-action that use engaging resources and tactile/visual support such as 'objects of reference', pictures, symbols and cards to help them orientate themselves towards participation.

 10.5 Online reading for Chapter 13 (Points 13.2 and 13.4)

Learning to share interest
Fig 4.1 depicts many learning to learn skills, which include:

- Sharing touching and handling

- Sharing focus on discrimination in objects and pictures

- Sharing following sequences of movement or action

- Sharing making groups and arrangements

- Sharing making changes

Developing skills such as:

- Appreciating object and background separation

- Tracking

- Developing awareness of object permanence

- Observing groups

- Comparing

- Matching

- Making and describing sequences

Notes

1 Porter, J. (2016) Introducing magnitude representation with Millie Moreorless, a digital game for children with Down syndrome. *SLD Experience* 75, 21–27

2 RNIB. Social inclusion in the early years, www.rnib.org.uk/sites/default/files/social_inclusion_early_years%5BJJ%5D.docx

3 Download Vision for Doing at: www.ssc.education.ed.ac.uk/resources/vi&multi/visionbook.pdf

4 Aitken, S. & Buultjens, M. (1992) *Vision for Doing*. Edinburgh: Scottish Sensory Centre. Moray House Publications, www.ssc.education.ed.ac.uk/resources/vi&multi/vfdh/vfdtoc.html

5 RNIB (2011) *Focus on Foundation*. Third edition. London: RNIB, www.rnib.org.uk/sites/default/files/focus_on_foundation_0.pdf

6 Though it is essentially intended as an assessment tool.

7 McLinden, M. & McCall, S. (2002) *Learning through Touch*. London: David Fulton.

8 Meares, O. (1980) Figure/ground, brightness contrast, and reading disabilities. *Visible Language* 14(1): 13–29.

9 Irlen, H. (1999) Scotopic sensitivity syndrome and the Irlen lens system. Autism Research Institute website, www.autism.com/understanding_irlens

10 Caldwell, P. (2013) Sensory distortions in autism, http://network.autism.org.uk/knowledge/insight-opinion/phoebe-caldwell-sensory-distortions-autism

11 Isaacs, P. (2016) Visual perception in autism, http://network.autism.org.uk/knowledge/insight-opinion/visual-perception-autism

Hearing

The range of hearing difficulties

Hearing loss can occur in a number of ways. Historically, it often went undetected, but screening of newborns has improved the situation. However, it remains an often-veiled disability, and even in the special classroom we can be unaware that some children are not hearing well.

Physical hearing loss

The majority of conductive hearing losses related to the physical workings of the ear arise from congenital conditions that relate to genetic syndromes, but around 25% are the result of non-genetic causes. Temporary infections like glue ear can be short term or intermittent, but sometimes become long term. Children with epilepsy also suffer intermittent hearing disruption, which can have serious effects if their petit mal episodes are frequent.

Neural hearing difficulties

As with vision, there are also cases caused by neural difficulties, often associated with attention disorders such as autism and ADHD, where the hearing difficulty is related to the brain's translation of sound into nerve impulses. In such cases, children may initially pass hearing tests, and yet struggle with understanding what people say. Sometimes these problems are not noticed until concerns about the child's language and behaviour are raised, by which time they have started on a cycle of disadvantage in communication and social skills (Musiek, 2010).[1]

 11.1 See online reading for more on the incidence of hearing losses

Difficulties that arise from hearing loss

Children with physical (conductive) hearing loss will generally experience sounds as quieter or muffled and, dependent upon severity, this will affect their attention to language and their ability to respond to, understand or replicate it. Sometimes hearing aids are used for children with conductive losses, but there are often problems managing them with special children. Profound deafness is sometimes treated with cochlear ear implants, but special children are still likely to need support.

Both conductive and neural losses will result in some of the following difficulties:

- *Auditory discrimination*: difficulty identifying, comparing or distinguishing between sounds. For example, 'sixty' and 'sixteen' can sound very similar, leading to errors in identification and pronunciation and, later, to difficulty with phonics.

- *Auditory figure–ground discrimination*: inability to focus on the important sounds in a noisy setting (e.g. not being able to follow the teacher's voice amidst the hubbub of the classroom).

- *Auditory memory*: inability to recall what you've heard, either straight away or later, in some cases even being unaware you don't remember.

- *Auditory sequencing*: confusing the order of sounds or words – a child saying "efelant" may be a common trait, but if it persists, it may indicate a problem. This is sometimes hidden because children who find it hard to be understood tend to not speak and pressuring them will not help.

Though causes differ widely, some of the options for helping children learn ways of overcoming sensory difficulties share common ground in multisensory learning.

Some thoughts about teaching related to hearing difficulties

In addition to passing on spoken information, hearing has some important functions that help the child's orientation:

Sound draws our attention to direction – it is very evident that sound makes us aware of direction because we so often turn towards it to locate its source.

Sound draws our attention to space – volume and tone also give us unconscious information about distance and space.

Sound draws our attention to changes – we are alerted to the pattern of events and time through experience of starting and ending sounds that use intonation, volume and alternation.

Toleration – for some pupils, teaching may need to work on helping them tolerate, manage and enjoy sounds in their environment.

Focus – some pupils may need support to focus on listening or imitating sound, separating sounds from the background or alternating attention between sources.

 11.2 Online reading includes some thoughts and ideas about teaching related to hearing difficulties

A whole view of sound – not just the ears

Evelyn Glennie is a world-renowned orchestral percussionist who has been profoundly deaf since the age of 12. She says, "Most of us know very little about hearing even though we do it all the time," in her Hearing Essay (1993)[2] and TED talk entitled 'How to Truly Listen' (2007). She explains that sound is vibrating air converted into signals, and the ear is not the only sense that can detect vibration, so she includes the role of other senses in making and experiencing sound. Although we are not usually conscious of it, we are all using more than our ears to 'listen', and there are many avenues of sensory stimulation we can include in the rhythms of our teaching actions to promote hearing in the widest of senses, including vibration, movement, touch and visual experience.

Working with hearing impairment

Communication

The use of signing is common to compensate for hearing communication difficulties, particularly Makaton or Signalong, which are intended to match the cognitive abilities of special children better than semantic sign languages. For some pupils, a prime purpose of this is as a means of focusing on spoken word structure, to emphasise turn taking and sequences of attention and action in sentences.

Likewise, objects of reference (RNIB, 2016)[3] are used to naturally precede the use of pictures, graphics and symbols as representations.

A good resource that can be downloaded is 'Supporting the Achievement of Hearing Impaired Children in Early Years Settings' from the National Sensory Impairment Partnership (NatSip/DfE, 2015).[4] Its advice covers environmental issues, teaching strategies, using visual aids such as timetables, picture labels, photo diaries, etc. It also covers key elements of non-verbal communication such as using facial expressions, gesture, touch and signing as alternatives to verbal interactions. The effectiveness of our teaching will depend on us using avenues of communication that generate motivation and curiosity that supports finding multisensory ways of 'listening' together.

Working on 'multisensory hearing'

Being profoundly deaf, hearing for Evelyn Glennie is a multisensory process. She tells us that vibration and sound are not separate, but part of the same channel. She also includes the role of other senses in experiencing sound, such as touch and pressure felt by the hands and arms as she plays, even the rhythmic pattern being established by movement, and the visual stimuli of watching the sticks ("the skin of the drum shimmering like leaves"). We may not be as highly tuned as Evelyn and we may use vibration and other senses less consciously, but nevertheless they are there as part of our multisensory experience, and we need to use them as much as possible for our very special pupils.

Imitation – movement and touch

Quite naturally, we are all multisensory communicators. Just as mime is a powerful artistic medium, our repertoire of non-verbal communication gestures are our means of establishing a framework for imitation – which is one of our most powerful teaching avenues.

Movement and touch are natural accompaniments to sound and are associated together in the development of mental patterns, so encouraging children to follow and use movements and gestures and to use touching are all ways of developing understanding.

Some ideas for promoting multisensory 'hearing'

- Emphasise communication and sound making with personal movements and mirroring facial expressions. Use physical and vocal call-and-response techniques.

- Physical rhythmic activities are related to brain development. Actions like clapping, beating and pointing are all intrinsic to sequencing and counting.

- Sound sources are also vibration sources – use resonant resources and microphones (e.g. beatboxing and sound-generating software on tablets) with speakers mounted on resonant surfaces.

 11.3 **Online reading expands on ideas for promoting multisensory 'hearing'**

Notes

1 Musiek, F. E. et al. (2010) American Academy of Audiology Clinical Practice Guidelines: Diagnosis, Treatment, and Management of Children and Adults with Central Auditory

Processing Disorder, https://audiology-web.s3.amazonaws.com/migrated/CAPD%20 Guidelines%208-2010.pdf_539952af956c79.73897613.pdf

2 Glennie, E. (1993) *Hearing Essay*, https://web.archive.org/web/20110410092415/http:// www.evelyn.co.uk/Evelyn_old/live/hearing_essay.htm

3 Hampson, J. (2014) The use of objects of reference as part of a multi-sensory communication system. RNIB Pears Centre, www.aacsig.org.uk/sites/default/files/presentations/ Poster%20OoR%20ISACC2014.pdf

4 NatSip/DfE (2015) Supporting the achievement of hearing impaired children in early years settings. London: DfE, www.google.co.uk/url?sa=t&rct=j&q=&esrc=s&source=w eb&cd=1&ved=0ahUKEwiz4K6qmYTPAhUICcAKHZRNB4AQFggoMAA&url=http%3 A%2F%2Fwww.ndcs.org.uk%2Fdocument.rm%3Fid%3D9422&usg=AFQjCNGyOd-HkZGI03RvjKJ9HsN6WAYdYA&bvm=bv.132479545,d.d2s

12 Touch and movement

It is through the touch senses that we make contact and have the power to change things. In the previous two chapters, the sense of touch has already made its presence felt as a companion to vision and hearing. In his 1934 essay 'In Praise of Hands', art historian Henri Focillion[1] said that vision is transitory – our most tangible knowledge about three-dimensional shapes and the nature of space requires touching, handling and moving. It was the stonemasons handling stone who originally developed the geometry to build the pyramids, from practical activity they became mathematicians.

 12.1 Online reading contains Focillion's elegant quote

Haptic touch – tactile and spatial awareness

Newborns are programmed to touch, but simply making contact is only part of the equation. Passive touch provides only static information such as temperature or hardness. Newborns need active movement, stroking and forming shapes with the fingers or feeling the forces of movement, pressing and reaching to find out about form, shape, size, weight and texture. This is called haptic touch – the name is from Greek and literally means 'to grasp something'.

The exploratory actions of the hand include;

- Lateral motion
- Pressure
- Enclosure
- Contour following

They are all coordinated with larger limb movement, as the skin's sense of touching works seamlessly with the senses of body position, force and movement (proprioception and vestibular senses) to develop our 'haptic perception'.

> **Proprioception, the vestibular sense and haptic perception in action**
>
> ■ As you walk into your own bathroom in the dark, without thought or looking, you raise your arm to exactly the right height and with an open palm your hand finds the light pull. You grasp it and pull with just the right force to turn on the light.
>
> ■ Or, you are blindfolded and have your hands open. Someone places a Lego brick on one palm and an egg on the other. As soon as you enclose your fingers you will know exactly what you have, and you know not to squeeze the egg too hard.

The whole body

In fact, hands are also only a part of this process, as touch is a sense of our whole body – the sense of the whole skin. We even sense touch inside our body, as our mouth is supersensitive – think of chewing and swallowing. It is through touching and being touched that we become aware of the boundaries of our own bodies and of other issues such as proximity and transfer of weight in movement. Even the soles of your feet tell you about the way you are moving. Rhythm of movement is a root of mathematical knowledge, as well as dancing. Yet we tend to take how the typical child develops their body map and awareness of space for granted, but as consciousness of conditions like dyspraxia grows, its importance is being increasingly recognised.

A fundamental sense for mathematics

In two previous chapters about physical skills, I described how children's patterns of physical actions develop into 'thinking' – schema. It may be self-evident that handling, touching and moving develop practical knowledge about objects, space, shape, weight, etc. But it is also the case that developing number knowledge has beginnings in touch and movement. We can see signs of this in the form of an infant's inclination to point, which eventually develops into itemising, sequencing and counting, and gradually progresses into more ideas. In later chapters, I will discuss the neurological connections between finger manipulation and representations of number, as hand skills are directly associated with the evolution of mathematical knowledge (Butterworth, 1999).[2] Typical children participate in a great deal of manipulative play and finger patterning, which enhance neurological development and connect to the mathematical language that is provided by adults.

When there are difficulties

Many SLD pupils have difficulties that affect the ease with which they move or handle objects and develop ideas through schema. Needing to concentrate on physical action reduces their motivation and the fluency of their learning. It is our role as teachers to fire their curiosity and inspire manipulation practice, alongside stimulating thinking through our own participation and commentary. Practical activities and games are our best medium of teaching. There is an example of a simple game we called 'Robot Grabber' described in the online reading. There are other games throughout the book – it is important to recognise that the manipulation and movement within them is in itself important to mathematical learning.

 12.2 Online reading includes a description of a game of Robot Grabber

Some very special issues

Working with children with profound learning difficulties
PLD children are often dependent on special seating and have visual impairments, closed hands and difficulty reaching out, so they are deprived of independent stimuli for haptic perception. So, our teaching must provide environments and experiences that develop their active curiosity in the pleasure of exploring with us. In the words of Penny Lacey – *enjoy yourself with the children* – but always implicit in her teaching was *know what you are doing and why*. Another of the inspirational teachers who has books full of practical teaching ideas, two of which are particularly relevant to this current topic, is Flo Longhorn (2000[3] and 1993[4]). A casual observer uninformed of how sensory systems develop might see the process of trailing a feather along a child's arm as merely tickling, but if you are a teacher who is aware that such trailing triggers neural pathways that refine body awareness, then you can be capable of using that technique purposefully. You can observe reactions, adapt actions and communicate with your pupil. The same is true of a social session involving wearing and swapping hats of different sizes, including cool hats and silly hats. Making choices gives children awareness of their head positions and movement and experience of language related to proximity and position, turn taking, differences and consequences of size and sequences of action, etc.

 12.3 Online reading contains just a few sensory ideas from of Flo Longhorn

Understanding the developmental progress that children make as you teach is important, and readers will find an excellent developmental overview of developing manipulation skills and ideas for promoting them in Appendix 8 of the downloadable guidance booklet for 'Routes for Learning' (Welsh Assembly, 2006).[5] For teachers who would like guidance to start with, 'Tacpac' (www.tacpac.co.uk) is a well-tried resource that outlines structured sessions for developing bodily awareness. But there is also a new generation of PMLD practitioners who spell out the rationale behind sensory working with books, blogs and websites – go seek out

Jo Grace's book *Sensory Being for Sensory Beings* (2007),[6] as well as the websites Sensory Dispensary[7] and Sensory Spectacle.[8]

The power of the teacher's touch

In a seminal article 'Do Touch' by Dave Hewett (2007)[9] on the importance of staff providing *touch*,[10] he discusses extensive evidence on massage therapy and physical contact as being an intrinsic developmental stimuli for brain development. He unequivocally states that "It is imperative to make available warm meaningful physical" contact to people who not only have PMLD, but also those with SLD and autistic students.

About providing the experience of touch and movement

We should always ensure pupils feel secure about experiences of touch and movement. But sometimes including a sense of risk such as that which occurs in games and outdoor/forest school experiences has an important role in extending sensory processing. The benefits of rebound therapy[11] and hydro therapy are well documented. Wheelchair movement, standing and suspension swinging through space in slings are learning experiences that give some students rare real experience of space, sequence, rhythm, frequency and time. They provide powerful contexts for communication. Think how much poorer your world would be if you had never danced or been on a swing as a child.

Working with children's hands

There are students who have become tactile defensive. Remember that their immobility may cause them pain. Whilst we need to improve their intentional mobility and manipulation, we must avoid creating negative responses.

Hand under hand support

Working with such children may sometimes require helping their manipulations, and in Chapter 7, I discussed direct support, but some practitioners seek alternative ways of working to promote independent action, working in a more mutual, sharing fashion. In 'Talking the Language of the Hands to the Hands', Barbara Miles (2003)[12] gives 13 suggestions for working with the hands to develop 'tactile intelligence'.

 12.4 Online reading includes examples of working with the hands to develop haptic perception

Later chapters will include much more detail about how children learn about numbers through the hands and fingers.

Notes

1 Focillion, H. (2013, first edition 1934) In praise of hands. In: *The Life of Forms in Art.* New York: Zone Books.

2 Butterworth, B. (1999) *What Counts – How the Brain is Hardwired for Maths.* New York: Simon & Schuster.

3 Longhorn, F. (2000) *Numeracy for Very Special People.* Catalyst Education Resources.

4 Longhorn, F. (1993) *Planning a Multisensory Massage Programme for Very Special People.* Catalyst Education Resources.

5 Routes for Learning (2006) Additional guidance, Appendix 8. Cardiff: Welsh Assembly, www.complexneeds.org.uk/modules/Module-2.1-Planning-to-meet-needs/All/downloads/m05p080b/routes_for_learning_additional_guidance.pdf

6 Grace, J. (2017) *Sensory Being for Sensory Beings – Creating Enchanting Sensory Experiences.* London: Routledge.

7 Sensory Dispensary, https://sensorydispensary.blogspot.co.uk

8 Sensory Spectacle, www.sensoryspectacle.co.uk

9 Hewett, D. (2007) Do touch. *Physical Support for Learning* 22(3), 116–123.

10 He also outlines guidelines for safeguards.

11 http://reboundtherapy.org

12 Miles, B. (2003) Talking the language of the hands to the hands. National Center on Deaf Blindness. Western Oregon University, http://documents.nationaldb.org/products/hands.pdf

13 Attention

The tool that makes sense of senses

Our powers of attention are important both as the beginning of learning experiences and as part of maintaining them. Attention is a root process of curiosity. It is often thought of as '*concentrating*' on information, but to be useful there has to be a balance of finding and focusing, seeking and filtering information so that we can maintain a useful path of thinking.

Seeking information

Attention involves both the conscious and unconscious mind working at various levels. For example, as we walk into the bakery, all our senses are absorbing stimuli that compete and combine. We are delightfully conscious of some of them as we savour the smells and colours, and we may even consciously register a sense of hunger that they trigger.[1] But at the same time, other senses are working unconsciously (e.g. our sight has automatically adjusted to the change of light, our proprioception adjusts our walking movement as we walk to the counter). Through all this, to be efficient, we have to manage sensory workload, balancing focus and distraction as we shift between conscious and unconscious information.

Filtering and being selective

Selective attention

At the same time that our senses are feeding our perceptions, the processes of attention are making sure that we are not overloaded. We use *selective attention* so that a stimulus will only be selected and rise to conscious thinking if something within it seems important enough, but we are continually scanning and will pick out things, such as the moment you notice your name in a background conversation; you will refocus, at least momentarily, to check it out.

These facets of attention illustrate an important point – *we are able to perceive the world not exactly as it is, in all its competing chaos, but as it is useful to us.* We use attention to focus – unless of course we have sensory processing difficulties that disrupt the balance of these seeking/evaluating and filtering processes.

Sharing attention

Learning from others

Developing the ability to attend begins in the womb. It is the outcome of the natural drive to use our sensory perceptual skills. For example, we are attracted to look at contrasting colours or to track moving objects or sounds. We follow the urge to reach and touch. Initially, the direction of infant attention is haphazardly dominated by how attractive competing stimuli are, but usually sharing attention with adults guides children's random sensory explorations towards sustaining attention usefully – and becoming aware of learning with other people.

Learning to share – the pointing finger

Even the simple act of a child's pointing is taken as a sign of cognitive ability. Psychologists like Elizabeth Bates (1976)[2] and many that followed have debated its roles in the development of language and thinking. They have discussed how the intentions of 'imperative pointing', which is a means of telling someone what you want, evolves into 'declarative pointing', which is a means of sharing attention. In so doing, much of the debate has revolved around the extent of children's theory of mind, and in particular Simon Baron-Cohen (1993)[3] has related this to autism. But many children with special needs have difficulty with either the physical act or the awareness of pointing, and it may be another of those fundamentally simple skills that we need to find ways of teaching.

Some ideas might include index finger exercises using:

- Finger massage and fingertip touching

- Modelling and assisted touching, textures with holes and knobbles and finger tapping

- Choosing – using pictures and screens and objects

- Button pressing – activation of toys and apps

- Finger toys for pointing – puppets and the witch finger extensions you can buy around Halloween

- Finger toys for pushing or tapping – finger skateboards

- Finger painting and tracing – art and apps

When there are difficulties

Almost all children with special educational needs (at the levels that this book deals with) have some degree of difficulties with attention. The roots are in the disruption of their sensory systems by physical or neural difficulties as outlined in earlier chapters.

 13.1 Online reading lists some conditions that are related to attention difficulties

The range of conditions is wide and many children have their own cocktails of symptoms. So, while there are common threads, there are also differences that can seem like polar opposites. For example, an under-responsive deaf–blind student may be withdrawn and tactile defensive, whilst a hyperactive sensory craver may be a whirlwind seeking excessive tactile or oral stimulation.

 13.2 Online reading describes various effects of neurological differences

There are two key areas for helping them learn to learn more effectively:

▦ Improving coordination of sensory processing

▦ Developing interaction skills

These are intertwined because participation together in physical activities that practice processing skills also develops experience of interaction.

Sensory coordination

Sometimes, gaining the child's participation demands the skilful cultivation of interaction by adults. When it can be gained, activities such as gross motor games, fine motor activities or therapeutic activities such as massage all play motivating roles in sensory development. Plenty of experiences like baking, drumming, balance games, track toys, mark making and page turning are all engaging and have mathematical elements to them.

The mind map in Fig. 13.1 gives a broad picture of activities in which adults and children can participate together, developing joint attention. When working, it is important to bear in mind that the aims include:

▦ Developing physical skills

▦ Awareness of sharing looking and listening to focus on activity

▦ Developing pointing

- Developing curiosity

- Discrimination

- Selection

- Anticipation

- Persistence

- Inclination towards problem solving

- Developing the child's desire to initiate social action

 13.3 Online reading lists some sources of teaching ideas

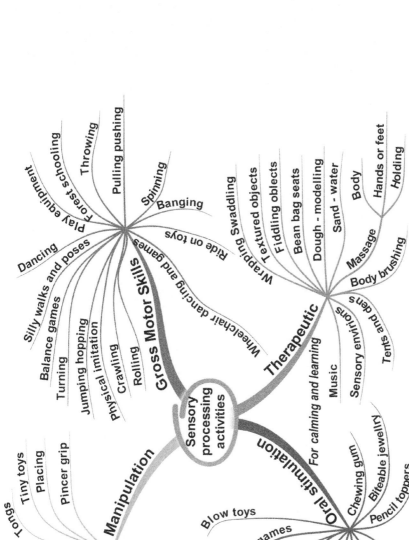

Figure 13.1 Sensory processing activities

Developing interaction skills

A vital outcome of participating together in sensory processing games is to develop playful partnerships that teach children how to act as 'initiators' and 'responders' as they start to realise things like:

■ They can generate actions from other people.

■ They can gain information from other people.

■ They can change things and have some control in their environment.

■ They are learning to learn.

One example occurred with a hypersensitive teenager who rarely made eye contact, but one day became fascinated when I put on a pair of white cotton gloves. He started to want to look at them – this was a teaching opportunity. It is described in more detail in the online reading, where there is also another example of working with Davina, who has complex learning difficulties. In an improvised sensory environment, we were able to engage her in turn taking and serve-and-return communication.

 13.4 Online reading illustrates examples of learning to learn

Notes

1 Hunger is one of the 'interoception' senses of internal organ function that detect responses for the regulation of our body. Some others are thirst, respiration, heart rate and elimination. Not often listed in diagnoses of disorders affecting education, they may actually have profoundly disturbing effects (e.g. creating anxieties or unusual desires, such as keeping moving to maintain excitement of heart beat or eating disorders).

2 Bates, E. (1976) *Language in Context: The Acquisition of Pragmatics*. New York: Academic Press.

3 Baron-Cohen, S. (1993) From attention–goal psychology to belief–desire psychology: the development of a theory of mind, and its dysfunction. In: S. Baron-Cohen, H. Tager-Flusberg & D. J. Cohen (Eds), *Understanding Other Minds: Perspectives from Autism. First edition* (pp. 59–82). Oxford: Oxford University Press.

14 Perception

Making sense of sensation

Attention and perception are our information processing tools. They work together – attention works at seeking and sorting sensory information, whilst perception is for making 'sense' of it. Perception works rapidly without conscious thought – as our senses scan around us, information is received and our brain relates it to all our memories of similar experiences, from which we make generalisations of what we are seeing, hearing, feeling, etc., using all of our prior knowledge (e.g. a certain kind of shape will make us think 'teapot'). So how we interpret sensory input is influenced by our expectations, and typically children develop a fund of perceptual ideas. The more experience we have, the more sophisticated our expectations can be.

Perception and mathematical learning

Core knowledge

All aspects of mathematical learning that have practical application in life depend upon us having the perceptions of objects, groups, shapes, spaces and time, etc.

In Chapter 4, I explained that psychologists have observed that typical children have perceptual knowledge even at birth. Elizabeth Spelke (Spelke & Kinzler, 2007)[1] has observed babies using what she calls 'core knowledge' in the first days of life, and those capabilities underpin everything children go on to learn later.

Perceptual core knowledge includes:

- *Object representation* – infants are able to separate objects and people from the background. They can perceive the boundaries of objects and appreciate that they can move.[2]

- *Geometric spatial awareness* – newborns have a degree of depth perception and also show interest in the contrast of edges and planes. Using vision and touch helps them build their three-dimensional understanding of the objects, spaces and positions of things around them.[3]

- *Number sense* – in the first days of life, infants can notice differences when they look at small groups of one to four things. They remember even when the groups are presented separately! Obviously, they don't *know* which is *more* or that they have names, but such perceptual number sense is a root skill of practical thinking, such as seeing differences to make comparisons or choices. How it leads to ideas about number we will discuss in later chapters.

 14.1 Online reading explains that core knowledge is the essence of everyday life skills

It may be that for some children with very special needs, core knowledge or the development of the skills from it is disrupted, in which case we need to try to find ways to promote the development of perceptual skills that mainstream teachers usually take for granted. For some very special pupils, this may apply to fundamental spatial perception, but Jordan and Dyson also relate it to difficulties encountered by cognitively able students with dyscalculia (Jordan & Dyson, 2014).[4]

Building on core knowledge

Some of the processes that both derive from and build on core knowledge are inherent in actions that occur as part of our everyday lives, but we need to consciously promote them during practical activities and games with special pupils. They might include perceptual skills dealing with real things:

- *Using depth perception* – experiences of distances for moving or reaching by judging relative sizes and dealing with motion.

- *Differentiating features* – separating and discerning what are the important elements – foreground separating background and so on – in any sensory mode.

- *Developing perceptual constancy* – identifying objects from different angles or positions.

- *Observation* – observing and recognising similarities and differences for choosing matching and sorting.

- *Placing* – appreciating processes of placing objects, which can lead to tracking, ordering and sequencing.

- *Grouping* – extending natural propensities to collect and arrange things.

- *Redistribution* – dealing with rearrangements of groups, appreciating conservation of number, etc.

- *Tracking* – following the movement of objects (or other stimuli), which is associated with developing appreciation of both cause and effect, object permanence and scanning that is part of counting.

- *Completing* – being able to make sense of incomplete or changing objects, images or events, which might include visual, tactile or kinaesthetic memories of objects, groups or spaces, sounds of communication or rhythm of music.

- *Connecting to meaning* – connecting real things to memories, linking things to representations such as pictures, symbols or symbolic objects, as well as spoken words to meaning.

- *Corresponding and adapting* new stimuli to existing knowledge and refining and making new ideas.

Perceptual tendencies

There are some tendencies of perception that are most often described in relation to visual information (e.g. dealing with pictures, graphics, text, etc.), but there are equivalences in other senses. The tendencies can be useful or problematic.

We use some tendencies to identify things or patterns:

- *Figure ground* – identifying foreground image or sound.

- *Closure* – completing whole images or auditory assumption.

- *Effects of proximity on judging size* – or volume on distance.

- *Continuity* – tendency to track along lines or sound sequences.

- *Proximity or similarity* tend to make us group things together.

 14.2 Online reading includes extensive examples of perceptual tendencies

But these tendencies can also cause disturbances

These tendencies can be bound up in neural processing disruptions, particularly when associated with visual stresses such as glare or contrast[5]. In such circumstances, they can lead to misperceptions, like text moving on the page or difficulty discriminating between similar figures such as '6' and '0', '2' and '5' or '6' and '9', or reversals such as reading '14' and '41', etc.[5] Difficulties with directional tracking and horizontal or vertical sequences can also cause misperceptions.

More acutely, the effects can be so disorientating that they generate distress or aversion (e.g. with strongly patterned carpets or vertical blinds casting patterned shadows on work surfaces).

Developing multisensory 'looking'

The pioneers of early years education like Froebel and Montessori all recognised that children need to develop purposeful, multisensory 'looking' using strategies that combine visual and auditory exploration with physical reaching and manipulation, moving themselves and things. An interesting perspective is illustrated by the case below.

An experience of distance perception

Gregory and Wallace (1963)[6] reviewed the case of an articulate man who had been very partially sighted but was given vision by an operation. They reported he could recognise objects that he had touched whilst he was blind (e.g. objects in rooms and the window frame), but was unable to interpret distant views or understand height when looking down from a high window.

He had concepts of rooms and objects because he had tactile, kinaesthetic and vestibular memory maps relating to mobility in limited spaces. These concepts may have been supported by other sensory information, like the resonance and echo that offer distance and quality clues for hearing that are akin to visual size, clarity, brightness and perspective clues. From this, we may draw the inference that it is beneficial to use experience from *all* senses to perceive the world, and this reinforces all that has been said in previous chapters about the importance of multisensory working.

Teaching opportunities

Perception is part of the general processes of living, but it becomes a particular part of learning mathematics when it is dealing with recognising and differentiating quantities, numerals, shapes and spaces. There are many high-tech avenues for developing perceptual skills – tracking lights or sounds in sensory rooms and using computers and tablets or projectors. But we should not forget that perceptual skills are in constant use and opportunities for refining them abound in everyday life and in all kinds of play. Touching, being touched and moving are primary sources of learning. Experience of being touched is fundamental to developing body image – through which all other dimensions are compared. Movement experience, feeling direction and speed are intrinsic to our spatial perceptions.

Experiences such as feeling the sizes and weights of objects, finding hidden or partially hidden things or watching or making arrangements and rearrangements of groups are all relevant as teaching opportunities. Resources such as Tacpac[7] tap into this. Even simply sharing books, pictures or objects provides an exercise in perception (e.g. looking into pictures to find the main objects, following patterns using visual or auditory memory, matching, sorting, tracing and copying are all processes in which perceptions are stretched).

Here are just a few simple ideas and themes that can exercise perception:

■ Items hidden in sand, rice, oats, pasta or foam – small lost objects or gradually revealing larger pictures

■ Hiding – or getting in and out of spaces

■ Using torches for finding and tracking – regular and ultraviolet LED torches

■ Wrapping and unwrapping – not only things but yourself

■ Feely bags and blindfold guessing – or tracking

■ Versions of sound Lotto

■ Making trails along lines (e.g. with stickers, action figures or train tracks)

■ Stacking, building, tiling and nesting

■ Rapid identification games – with objects, pictures or dot patterns

During the forthcoming chapters on the development of play, readers will find more examples of opportunities that inherently exercise sensory discrimination and refine the use of perceptual skills.

When we reach the chapters on number sense and discuss dyscalculia, there will be more discussion about encouraging children to use perceptual skills to identify groups and make comparisons and estimations.

 14.3 Online reading includes some useful sources to inform your thinking and inspire your teaching

Notes

1 Spelke, E. S. & Kinzler, K. D. (2007) Core knowledge. *Developmental Science* 10(1), 89–96.
2 They are also aware that people are agents who can do things.
3 Ultimately, understanding of space, shape, measures and practical geometry are built on these foundations.
4 Jordan, N. & Dyson, N. (2014) *Number Sense Interventions*. Baltimore: Paul H. Brookes Publishing, Inc.
5 I have already noted the growing body of opinion that advocates for the use of Irlen lenses or tinted overlays to reduce contrast effects.
6 Gregory, R. L. & Wallace, J. G. (1963) Recovery from early blindness. *Experimental Psychology Society Monographs*. No. 2, www.richardgregory.org/papers/recovery_blind/recovery-from-early-blindness.pdf
7 http://tacpac.co.uk

Part 3
Processes of learning

15 Introducing the processes of learning

Developing exploration and refinement

As we observe children, it often delights us to see some new feature of physical skill or language appear. Learning springs from their inquisitive play, their interest in a stimulus and responding in order to cause effects.

The child's own awareness that their actions can affect things (contingency awareness) is the beginning point for active thinking and learning. This has been emphasised by many writers – and particularly for our special pupils in 'Routes for Learning'[1] and by Penny Lacey (2009).[2]

Such exploratory learning happens in the course of everyday life, and usually children pass through its processes so fluently that they are thought of as instinctive, not taught. Perhaps it is because play is usually so natural that the conventional curriculum takes it for granted and doesn't include it beyond early years. But there is more to play than just natural exploration, and if we want to know more about the ways that special children 'learn to learn' and how they develop 'thinking', we need to look more closely at how they explore. As so many writers have told us, they play to learn.

This book is about 'mathematics' and thinking for children with very special needs. But I will spend a long time talking about 'play' because the mathematics that children need to learn is involved in exploring and applying results as they live life. Life maths is one of their main 'doing and thinking' tools.

A cycle of learning through exploration

If we were to watch typical children as they worked through the processes of play – or any practical learning – we would notice there is a cycle of phases of learning.

- Children's learning starts with perceptions, inquisitiveness and awareness of stimulation and situation.

- They move on to responding by examining or using investigative action.

■ This extends into problem solving in a spirit of trial and error or improvement.

■ This then leads to making interpretations and new understanding that fits alongside or extends previous knowledge.

■ When the cycle is completed, children explore again. The cycle is repeated as an ongoing wave – the more curious and persistent they are, the more effective they will be as learners.

The learning cycle of play is illustrated in the Fig. 15.1.

Play and the profile of engagement

Fig. 15.1 also illustrates the relationship of play with forms of engagement in learning that are described in 'The Engagement Profile' (CLDD, 2011), which is a tool for observing the nature of children's engagement in activities. It has been recommended by the Rochford Review (2016) as a good way to evaluate learning for children at early developmental levels. Its indicators of engagement observed are levels of *awareness, curiosity, investigation, discovery, anticipation, persistence and initiation.*

 15.1 Online reading includes notes on the engagement profile and a copy of its diagrammatic representation

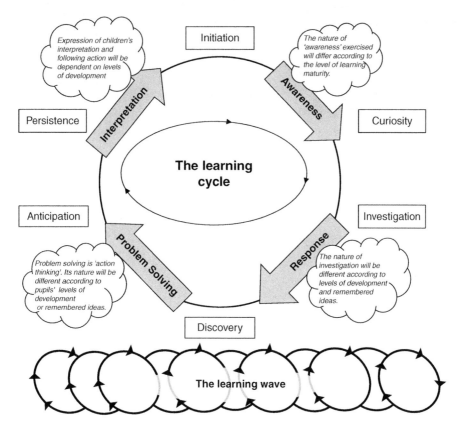

Initiation

Expression of children's interpretation and following action will be dependent on levels of development

The nature of 'awareness' exercised will differ according to the level of learning maturity.

Persistence

Interpretation

Awareness

Curiosity

The learning cycle

Anticipation

Problem Solving

Response

Investigation

Problem solving is 'action thinking'. Its nature will be different according to pupils' levels of development or remembered ideas.

The nature of investigation will be different according to levels of development and remembered ideas.

Discovery

The learning wave

Figure 15.1 The learning cycle and aspects of engagement

The cycle and its connection to curriculum organisation

The cycle interrelates with three '*characteristics of effective learning*' that are described in early years guidance (Early Education, 2012)[3]:

- Playing and exploring

- Active learning

- Creating and thinking critically

In recent years, special schools have recognised the relevance of these characteristics to developing a curriculum that:

1. Frees them from unsuitable age-related content in the National Curriculum
2. Delivers developmentally appropriate content

Examples where schools have put processes of play at the heart of their provision are:

- The Pre-Formal Curriculum at Fountaindale School (2014)[4]

- Castlewood School in collaboration with the late Penny Lacey (2016)[5]

Different levels of playing and learning

It is interesting to note how the essences of this cycle reoccur wherever a learning process is described. The same cycle is used to describe ostensibly different learning. For example, both the infant who learns to stack bricks and the scientist following a hunch pass through these phases. So, it is a description capable of working at different levels, and it does so for all our special pupils.

Children of different abilities are involved in the playing processes in different ways, depending on their developmental maturity. For some, their participation may be predominantly sensory, whilst others might focus on physical action and a few may be starting to use verbal observations and even starting to 'reason'.

All children work at sensory levels

Most extend sensory experience to concrete activity and reasoning motor exploration

Some continue with sensory and concrete experience but extend to use more abstract ideas

Figure 15.2 Levels of differentiation

In practice, the levels are not strictly defined – they are over-layered, and children cycle between layers as they acquire new skills and consolidate existing levels. Those who progress to higher levels still require sensory involvement as a relevant part of the learning experience.

Sometimes, classes in special needs settings can include pupils in all the layers and, where possible, it can often be beneficial to plan for socially inclusive learning activities so that pupils can participate together, each learning usefully at their own personal levels, benefiting from the power of peer modelling that communal learning can offer. For example, different children may achieve different learning from being in a sensory environment such as a forest school session. There is a lesson example below – and a more general table is available in the online reading.

 15.2 Online reading includes a table describing levels of engagement in life maths play (Table 15.1)

An example of children working together but at different levels of awareness

If a group of very special students are working together as part of an enterprise activity involving filling plant pots with compost to plant hyacinths to sell, they may be engaged in different ways.

PLD students – work at sensory levels.

■ They may be aware of the sensory properties of the soil and interested in participating in putting soil into the pots.

SLD students – extend sensory experience to concrete reasoning.

■ They may participate in the processes and understand the idea of filling.

Some students – continue with sensory and concrete experience, but extend to use more abstract ideas.

■ They may be aware that there is a need to fill a specific number of pots or conscious of the possibility of not having enough compost.

So we will be enabling them to develop different responses related to their different needs.

When there are difficulties in learning to play

In a contribution aptly entitled 'Playing to Learn or Learning to Play', Imray and Orr (2015)[6] noted no fewer than 22 reasons why, when they are left to their own devices, play does not come as naturally to our very special pupils as it does to their more typical peers. The list includes issues such as difficulties with manipulation, memory, concentration, generalising experience or stepping on from concrete to abstract thinking, as well as difficulties relating to social and communication skills. They make the suggestion that:

If the points are limiting factors which prevent the pupils from participating in play
then they are also the very experiences that are needed to enable them to learn to play.

During the coming chapters, I hope to illustrate more about how we can do this.

In her writing about teaching thinking to special children, Penny Lacey (2009)[7] wrote eloquently about the need to inspire curiosity and provoke play and real-life problem solving in ways that children would *enjoy* and be motivated by. Lilli Nielsen (1992)[8] showed us how to kick-start consciousness of cause and effect and create environments for independent exploration. There are other writers whose vision of typical development is relevant to the microscopic teaching we need to develop. For example, Vygotsky (1962, 1978)[9] highlighted how we need to assist their independent performance by scaffolding achievement and modelling steps forward, whilst Bruner's (1976)[10] work on peek-a-boo is fundamental to the beginnings of thinking. His work on using narrative thinking (1991)[11] emphasises how we learn to connect our memories and thoughts together.

 15.3 See online reading for a quick view of theories about learning and exploration

The following chapters will take us through thinking about many kinds of play because they are processes of learning that the conventional curriculum takes for granted and we need to know about them.

Notes

1 Routes for Learning – the important assessment tool for PMLD children developed by the Welsh Assembly (2006) recognises the importance of developing children's contingency awareness (their appreciation of cause and effect) as a beginning point of the child's ability to make choices, which is the beginning of active thinking.
2 Lacey, P. (2009) Developing the thinking of learners with PMLD. Reprinted in *PMLD Link* 27(2).
3 Early Education (2012) Development Matters in the Early Years Foundation Stage (EYFS). Non statutory guidance booklet. London: Early Education, www.foundationyears.org.uk/files/2012/03/Development-Matters-FINAL-PRINT-AMENDED.pdf
4 Fountaindale School. 'The Pre-formal Curriculum', www.fountaindale.notts.sch.uk/library/documents/The_new_preformal_curriculum_handbook_2014_v96WEB_VERSION.pdf
5 Castlewood School (2016), www.castlewood.coventry.sch.uk
6 Imray, P. & Orr, R. (2015) Playing to learn or learning to play. In: P. Lacey et al. (Eds), *The Routledge Companion to Severe, Profound and Multiple Learning Difficulties* (pp. 356–364). London: Routledge.
7 Lacey, P. (2009) Teaching Thinking in Special Schools. *SLD Experience* 54, 19–24.
8 Nielsen, L (1992) *Space and Self.* Denmark Sikon Press, www.ssc.education.ed.ac.uk/resources/vi&multi/lilli/lillibooks.html
9 Vygotsky, L. S. (1962) *Thought and Language,* London: Wiley. Vygotsky, L. S. (1978) *Mind in Society.* Cambridge, MA: MIT Press.
10 Bruner, J. S. & Sherwood, V. (1976) Peek-a-boo and the learning of rule structures. In: J. Bruner, A. Jolly & K. Sylva (Eds), *Play: Its Role in Development and Evolution* (pp. 277–287). Middlesex: Penguin.
11 Bruner, J. (1991) The narrative construction of reality. *Critical Enquiry* 18, 4.

16 Learning to play

From sensory exploration to social play

Sensory awareness is the starting point of the learning cycle and curiosity is the driving force of exploratory play. But it is a sense of social playfulness that predisposes children to seek social interaction and propels them from solitary exploration into social play and learning from others (Barnett, 1990).[1]

Typical children naturally extend from solitary into social play, but Imray and Orr (2015)[2] suggest that for many children with very special needs, interactive or social play doesn't occur spontaneously. They reflect on the journey that typical children make towards social play:

1. It starts with free enjoyment of the processes of exploration, using their senses to gather knowledge, as has been described in my previous chapters.
2. But as they do this, their experiences alongside other people teaches them that the processes of playing together have social patterns and structures that can be shared intentionally. They learn that social play can have aims and *products* (i.e. outcomes), such as achieving goals or winning.

When free play evolves to become social, it becomes a purposeful means of learning from other people – and children become capable of being conscious of what they can learn (Simons, 1977).[3] All too often, special children are unaware of this.

Pupils who have poor attention and short-term memories have difficulty making sense of social language (Hulme & McKenzie, 1992).[4] So although they may enjoy sensory, object or manipulative play, it tends to remain solitary, and they fail to connect the experiences from free play to social or cooperative thinking. Imray and Orr (2015)[5] suggest that for those pupils we need to deliberately organise structured social play in order to scaffold their learning. They recommend using structured play to teach special children about social interaction. As it happens, social play and games are a hotbed of opportunities for modelling mathematical life skills and knowledge.

Good contexts for scaffolding learning

Learning from reality

As Imray and Orr[6] note the idea of providing structured play experience *before* free play may seem to turn the Western world's idea that play first develops through exploration on its head. But observing and imitating the real actions of adults is actually a fundamental way that children develop. Domestic imitation is a prevalent form of play in many cultures (Holmes, 2013).[7] Whilst we do think of children *learning* as they 'work' in the garden or kitchen alongside us, perhaps we could give more credence to *participating together* as a school technique of teaching. Whenever children watch, they are learning. The ways that communication skills, social behaviour and knowledge spring from adult participation with children is so natural that adults are often not conscious they are using '*teaching*' techniques.

However, it may help our teaching of special children if we refine and emphasise our skills of modelling and language as we work in parallel with them as our apprentices.

The mind map in Chapter 2 illustrated the many contexts in everyday life where mathematics occurs, and all of these are also opportunities for practical and playful modelling. They include:

- Social activities and routines

- Personal care routines

- Domestic and practical activities

- Fitness and sport

- Participation in cultural activities

- Creative expression

 16.1 Online reading describes an example of maths learning opportunities that happen in a baking session

Learning in games

Watson and Corke[8] have noted, "The urge to have playful interactions based on timing and rhythm appears to be an innate sense," and perhaps the inclination towards games springs from core communication knowledge.

Participating in games exposes children to sharing a wide range of physical and social communication skills in very motivating ways. During the excitement of a game, children develop expectations and spontaneous problem solving. There are lots of opportunities for repeated modelling and practice of skills. They also include experience of mathematical ideas such as winning, gaining, losing, sequencing, distributing, etc. The mind map in Fig. 16.1 illustrates some of these social and communication skills – as well as some of the maths skills that occur in games.

Devising games

Games are not always formal affairs with complex rules; sometimes they are simple playful interactions, but fundamental social rules like turn taking can evolve from participating in them. Sometimes games can spring from experiences of chance like tossing a coin or turning a card. (Please bear in mind that games of chance, particularly if they involve winning and losing, may be taboo for children from some communities.)

Games can arise from sensory physical exchanges, such as clapping together, or tests of skill that you may practise on your own or in competition with others, such as throwing or balancing. They may be devised for different contexts (e.g. a penalty shootout), they can be real, they can be improvised on a table or they may be an app on a tablet. There were suggestions about games in Chapter 7, and all the schema patterns discussed in Chapter 8 feature within games.

Some themes that are useful to include when devising games are:

■ *Sensory sharing* – developing shared attention to sensory experiences, objects or activities (e.g. handling things, giving and receiving, passing – one to one or group activities)

■ *Giving and receiving* – experiences of exchanging, collecting and distributing things

■ *Alternating activities* – turn taking actions and sounds

■ *Manipulation and play with objects and materials* – placing, arranging, filling, emptying, tearing and folding

■ *Constructions and tracks* – building and connecting

■ *Hiding and revealing* – develop problem solving, searching, memory and object permanence

■ *Sequential actions and consequences*

■ *Games of chance or choice* – roll of a dice, spinner, lucky dip, etc., generate anticipation – forms of scoring and collecting

■ *Games of skill* – using motor skill games to generate winning, losing, scoring, pursuing goals, etc.

 16.2 Online reading expands on themes that are useful to include when devising games

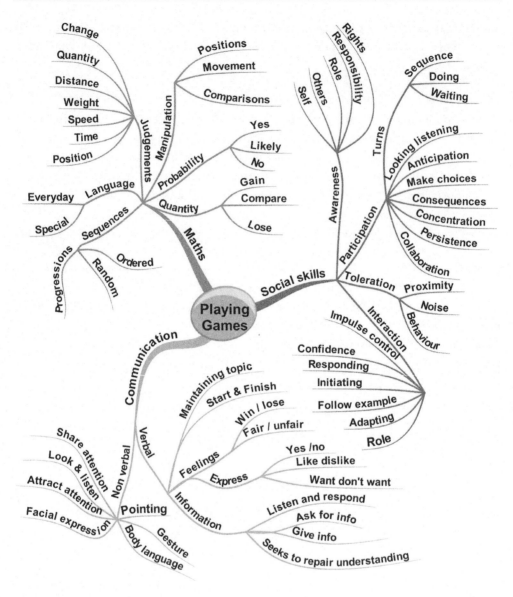

Figure 16.1 Skills involved in playing games

Levels of participation and learning

Games usually provide differentiated learning opportunities because in most contexts there are different levels of participation for different pupils, such as when a mixed group is involved in a creative art session making hand prints.

■ A sensory learner will be experiencing touch and manipulative and rhythmic movement control of the hands, as well as making one-to-one marks.

■ A solitary learner or onlooker will be benefitting from experience of working alongside others and taking turns in sequence.

■ Pupils who are social learners will experience all of the above, but may also be involved in taking turns, linear patterning, vocalising, counting words and thinking about counting.

Potential in technology

Exciting developments in technology open up new ways of playing. Using switch technology (which enables physically disabled children to make choices with multiple switches or limb or head movements) is well established. Nintendo Wii encourages physical limb movement, balance boards were discussed in Chapter 7 and online resources, programmable toys like Bee-Bot, iPads and other tablet apps are all proving their worth. The growing availability of eye gaze technology will be a game changer.

 16.3 See online resources for more about the potential of technology

About modelling

The importance of mutual interactions

Germinating play is not a process of instruction – it requires participation
There is no way to overestimate the importance of modelling in our facilitation techniques, but its use requires subtle skills. It's not just what you do – it's also the way that you do it. There is a danger of interpreting modelling as 'demonstration', with children watching while we show them what to do. With very special children, this can degenerate into doing things for them. So, it is worth thinking about how to use modelling strategies that might motivate and help children to be participators who learn to serve and return in activities and communication.

Mirroring
Physical imitation and modelling evolve from neurological roots of learning. There are mirror neurons in the brain that fire *both* when we act *and* when we observe another's actions (Keysers, 2010).[9] Even just watching creates signals in our corresponding muscles as though we were acting ourselves – it *couples* our perceptions to areas of muscular action.

Mirror neurons are the reason we reflect other people's gestures in conversations and why babies can rapidly develop the ability to imitate facial expressions. So, mirroring is not only part of our physical skills, but is also the biological root of communication and social skills – the very skills that are needed to enable children to learn to play.

It has been established that serve and return interactions with human partners shape the neural networks that are the communication architecture of the brain (Dawson & Fischer, 1994).[10] I believe this tells us that when we organise play experiences for children, it is also our job to be a participator. The strategies of 'intensive interaction' (Nind & Hewett, 2001),[11] which are becoming so important in our special schools, tap into related principles.

The importance of our playfulness

Establishing serve and return partnerships is important in nurturing play responses. Imray and Orr[12] reflected on suggestions from Trevarthen (1979)[13] and Stern (1985)[14] that *since responsiveness is the most essential trait of a play partner, the best teacher of play is one who responds to a companion's playfulness.* Their suggestions draw me to mentioning the importance of ideas discussed by Debby Watson and Margaret Corke (2015)[15] about developing *playfulness* in learners by being playful ourselves. They celebrate how skilled practitioners tune into their pupils' playfulness.[16] Can we bring an inclination to be playful into our teaching? Look at the box below, where the teacher uses balloons as a resource for counting experiences. Yes, it's a simple lesson, but full of fun, motivating learning potential.

An anecdote about a playful teacher

I have had some great lessons using whoopee cushions to create 'counting' events, so you can imagine my delight when Watson and Corke (2015)[17] provided a lovely example of a maths lesson for a group of PLD pupils in which the teacher uses a balloon playfully.

Pauline the teacher makes a show of counting the huffs and puffs of breath it takes to blow up the balloon.

Later, she releases air slowly and teasingly in bursts of three squeaks for each learner.

I can feel the attention in the room – and applaud the imagination that can see the potential for teaching listening skills, anticipation, self-regulation, pattern recognition and counting with this simple strategy.

When Liebermann (1977)[18] identified aspects of playfulness, his list of its components included 'spontaneous reactions', along with 'shared joy' and 'sense of humour'. Penny Lacey (2009)[19] also points us towards using creative, playful teaching to get special children to focus their attentions: "We need to demonstrate curiosity ourselves and (perhaps) even sabotage routines so that children begin to think."

What better message could my book have? Play with your pupils and make sure they enjoy you and that you enjoy your interactions with them.

Playfulness needs responses to turn it into learningfullness.

Notes

1 Barnett, L. (1990) Playfulness, definition design and measurement. *Play and Culture* 3, 319–336.

2 Imray, P. & Orr, R. (2015) Playing to learn or learning to play. In: P. Lacey et al. (Eds), *The Routledge Companion to Severe, Profound and Multiple Learning Difficulties* (pp. 356–364). London: Routledge.

3 Simons, C. (1977) Learning to play together. *British Journal of Special Education* 4(2), 17–19.

4 Hulme, C. & McKenzie, S. (1992) *Working Memory and Severe Learning Difficulties.* Hove: Laurence Erlbaum Associates.

5 Imray, P. & Orr, R. (2015) Playing to learn or learning to play. In: P. Lacey et al. (Eds), *The Routledge Companion to Severe, Profound and Multiple Learning Difficulties* (pp. 356–364). London: Routledge.

6 Imray, P. & Orr, R. (2015) Playing to learn or learning to play. In: P. Lacey et al. (Eds), *The Routledge Companion to Severe, Profound and Multiple Learning Difficulties* (pp. 356–364). London: Routledge.

7 Holmes, R. M. (2013) Children's play and culture. *Scholarpedia* 8(6), 31016, www. scholarpedia.org/article/Children%27s_play_and_culture

8 Watson, D. & Corke, M. (2015) Supporting playfulness in learners with SLD/PMLD. In: P. Lacey et al. (Eds), *The Routledge Companion to Severe, Profound and Multiple Learning Difficulties* (pp. 365–374). London: Routledge.

9 Keysers, C. (2010) Mirror neurons. *Current Biology* 19(21), R971–R973.

10 Dawson, D. & Fischer, K. W. (Eds) (1994) *Human Behavior and the Developing Brain.* New York: Guilford Press.

11 Nind, M. & Hewett, D. (2001) *A Practical Guide to Intensive Interaction.* Kidderminster: British Institute of Learning Difficulties.

12 Imray, P. & Orr, R. (2015) Playing to learn or learning to play. In: P. Lacey et al. (Eds), *The Routledge Companion to Severe, Profound and Multiple Learning Difficulties* (pp. 356–364). London: Routledge.

13 Trevarthen, C. (1979) Communication and cooperation in early infancy. A description of primary intersubjectivity. In: M. Bullowa (Ed.), *Before Speech: The Beginning of Interpersonal Communication* (pp. 321–348). Cambridge: Cambridge University Press.

14 Stern, D. (1985) *The Interpersonal World of the Infant.* New York: Basic Books.

15 Watson, D. & Corke, M. (2015) Supporting playfulness in learners with SLD/PMLD. In: P. Lacey et al. (Eds), *The Routledge Companion to Severe, Profound and Multiple Learning Difficulties* (pp. 365–374). London: Routledge.

16 They describe a session where Sam uses mirroring to promote communications from Peter, a pupil with autism (p. 367).

17 Watson, D. & Corke, M. (2015) Supporting playfulness in learners with SLD/PMLD. In: P. Lacey et al. (Eds), *The Routledge Companion to Severe, Profound and Multiple Learning Difficulties* (pp. 365–374). London: Routledge.

18 Liebermann, J. N. (1977) *Playfulness: Its Relationship to Imagination and Creativity.* New York: Academic Press.

19 Lacey, P. (2009) Teaching thinking in SLD schools. *SLD Experience* 54, 19–24.

17 | There are many ways of playing

Phases of development from roots of play

There is an observable sequence in the phases of play that children usually pass through on their journey from birth to social play. It is developmental, but does not form a hierarchy in which later forms *replace* the earlier stages; in fact, as it grows, there are overlaps between types and they continue to coexist in children's repertoires, and we can even detect their elements in our adult behaviour.

All phases are important to very special pupils

When we are working with very special pupils, we need to continue to provide experiences that relate to *all* of the phases in parallel, because:

1. *Attunement* interactions are at the roots of the brain's social organisation and learning behaviours.

2. *Reflexes* – primitive reflexes integrate into deliberate actions of life and exploration.

3. *Sensory play* is at the root of developing environmental awareness, functional skills and information gathering.

4. *Solitary play* includes exploration, practice, refinement and comfort.

5. *Onlooker play* provides safe observation of other people's actions and ideas.

6. *Play that is becoming social – parallel and associative play* – provides experiences that open up socialisation and communication that expose children to other people's processes and actions and make them aware of other people's thinking.

<table>
<tr><th colspan="4">Phases of developing play</th></tr>
<tr><td rowspan="12">Across phases there are a variety of ways of playing that children can learn from.
Sensory – manipulative – gross motor-movement – domestic – practical – creative – competitive – pretend – musical – social</td><td colspan="2">Play at the beginning of learning</td><td rowspan="5">Beginning with learning process of play</td></tr>
<tr><td>Attunement</td><td>Establishing fundamental connections and interaction with people.</td></tr>
<tr><td>Reflex</td><td>Maturation of primitive (pre-intentional) reflexes to postural reflexes working towards intentional reaction.</td></tr>
<tr><td>Sensory Play</td><td>Developing skills of exploration with environment and people.</td></tr>
<tr><td>Solitary play</td><td>Developing practicing and applying skills.</td></tr>
<tr><td colspan="2">Play becoming more social</td><td rowspan="7">Working towards play with intentional aims or products.</td></tr>
<tr><td>Onlooker play</td><td>Learning from observing other children play.</td></tr>
<tr><td>Parallel Play</td><td>Playing separately but adjacent to others.</td></tr>
<tr><td>Associative play</td><td>Beginning to play alongside other children.</td></tr>
<tr><td>Cooperative play</td><td>Beginning to play with other children.</td></tr>
<tr><td>Social forms of play</td><td>Collaborative exploration – creative – dramatic.</td></tr>
</table>

Figure 17.1 Phases of developing play

7. *Cooperative play* widens the contexts available to play in and is the practice ground for applying social skills and learning about thinking and mutual problem solving.

Children with special needs do not make the transitions across these phases as easily as their peers. It will help our teaching if we understand about the subtleties of these phases so that we can create learning situations that help them make the best of exploration and support transition.

Phases of play

Attunement play

The interactive processes that establish attachment between children and caregivers are universally recognised to underpin well-being and confidence, which are essential for positive orientation towards any form of learning. Many parents and teachers spoke to Watson and Corke (2015)[1] about tuning into the 'spirit of playfulness' in their PMLD children. They said it was important in making them feel positive about helping their child's development. It is important to consider the development of such relationships as part of the mission of any special curriculum.

Serve and return
Developing the serve and return experiences that arise from mutual experiences of contact are processes that stimulate midbrain connections (Perry et al., 2000).[2] They are the essence of shared attention upon which any possibility of learning from others depends. They are also the roots of 'intensive interaction' strategies that are so important in special education (Hewett et al., 2015),[3] and it is quite poignant that while inspirational practitioners like Phoebe Caldwell (2008)[4] describe the processes of synchronising breathing patterns as powerful elements of developing attunement, breathing and the heart beat are also essences of the mathematical rhythms of human life.

Serve and return – mutual experiences that promote attunement

- Being held

- Alternating visual and vocal exchanges

- Tracking faces

- Sharing looking and tracking objects and sound

- Rocking, carrying and rhythmic moving (dancing)

- Hand touching and tracing

- The exercise of developing mutual hand movements

- Coming and going

17.1 Online reading includes an example attunement with Claire

Reflexes

Whilst not usually thought of as play, reflexes are the beginnings of action and all learning stems from reflex development. It begins during pregnancy and is seated in the brainstem. Infants are born with primitive reflexes required for survival – such as the physical actions used in birth itself, sucking and swallowing, etc.

 17.2 See online reading for more about reflexes

Physical problems
The movements of very young children are dominated by involuntary primitive reflexes, such as startling, but gradually, through their own movement, new circuits are stimulated, and integrated reflexes can be used for voluntary actions such as reaching, grasping, crawling, etc. Difficulties with this development are very evident in children with cerebral palsy or PMLD, who we need to support to develop intentional actions. Our role is to enable them to participate in sensory exploration.

Neural problems
Incomplete maturation of infant reflexes is also cited as affecting brain development and causing learning difficulties such as ADHD and others. Manipulation games, movement, music and massage provide sensory integration sessions and help to overcome these difficulties, as well as often encompassing mathematical experience.

Sensory play

A central theme of this book is that mathematics has sensory beginnings – and so does play. Ironically, some lists that describe the development of play don't even include 'sensory play', or in the past even talked about it as 'unoccupied play'. These days, we realise that the maturation of reflexes and voluntary actions, such as reaching, stroking and grasping, coupled with sensory examination become coordinated into purposeful exploration, from which ideas of cause and effect and schema develop. Activities of sensory play such as those outlined in Chapters 7 and 8 are a large part of that learning.

Remember, Einstein told us that his thinking had sensory beginnings and that "Play is the highest form of research." The breadth of ways in which aspects of sensory play contribute to practical mathematical knowledge is illustrated in Fig. 17.2.

It is worth remembering that sensory play never goes away – we even use it is as adults. It is usually a starting point for any new practical learning and is always necessary as the root system of ideas. But people often use it as a background to thinking or calming as they fiddle with things or doodle.

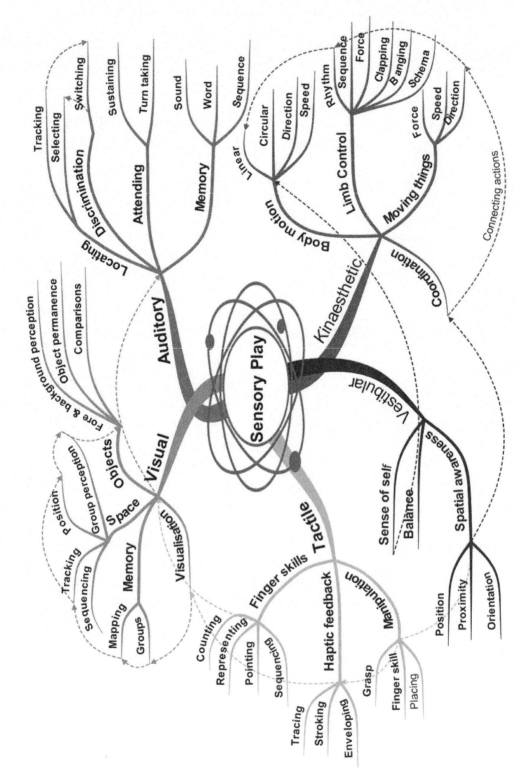

Figure 17.2 Sensory play is essential for mathematical development

Sensory play is practical

The growth of the sensory curriculum has led to many technological developments. Specifically designed sensory environments and high-tech sensory rooms are common in our special schools, and when used well they offer exciting possibilities. But play, which is the basis sensory exploration of typically developing children, is largely done with everyday objects, materials and commonplace toys, or even simply their own bodies. It can be in a kitchen or a forest – everywhere we use our senses. In the words of Flo Longhorn, Robert Orr or Richard Hirstwood, every room is sensory, and to quote the spirit in Fountaindale School's curriculum documents – any 'thing' can be a toy.

Typical children are driven by curiosity. They flow into sensory activity with ease and gain from a seemingly incessant willingness to practice. They are also inveterate communicators and they readily convert their physical practice into social discourse, with endless commentary: first naming; later describing action; and then questioning. But for special children, even initial exploration is often inhibited, as physical disabilities make fluent manipulation difficult or neural differences disrupt the usual channels of sensory examination. So sometimes it is difficult for sensory play to begin – or sometimes it goes into repetitive backwaters and fails to progress towards social interaction.

Chapter 7 described some approaches to promoting physical access for getting investigation started, but it is also important for us to recognise that it is sharing attention to things and communicating together that leads children to turn sensory experience into social knowledge. A major part of our teaching is in participating in play together, which leads us into the need to think about how children move from solitary sensory play to social play.

Solitary play

For typical children, much of the sensory play described above is individual or, as I described it in Chapter 4, '*personal exploration*'. This kind of playing and practising is prevalent before they are able to manage the social requirements of playing with others. But with typical children, we soon see that even in solitary play they start to apply purpose to objects, often playfully imitating adult actions (e.g. wrapping a doll with a blanket or feeding a stuffed toy). As this develops, the typical solo player may start to use private monologue, which illustrates their thinking, and if adults can 'join' in with it, it is possible that the child may learn something about both participating and absorbing information from others.[5]

Developing 'thought' through private dialogue is one of the many processes that typically developing children use so naturally that we hardly acknowledge it in our ideas about teaching, yet parallel dialogues have a strong track record in the development of language and thought, such as the role of 'parentese' and other forms of 'private speech' that were first outlined by Vygotsky and Luria (1929),[6] were expanded in Vgotsky's (1986)[7] classic text *Thought and Language* and have been part of the debates about language and thought ever since.

📝 **17.3 See online reading for more about parentese and private speech**

Sliding in mirroring and modelling

The teaching task in hand is to support the child in making the most of their play experience and in moving from solitary play towards more social discourse. When special children do not initiate communications about their play, we need to find ways by which they will accept us into participating with them in it. By sliding in, we can use forms of parallel dialogue to stimulate serve and return and generate communication. It gives us a chance to emphasise the content of experience being shared.

Forms of parallel language that can be used for modelling include:

- Parentese

- Speaking thoughts aloud

- Descriptive commentary

- Self-directive speech – used without directly addressing the child

- Speaking through objects

I will return to these in following paragraphs when I discuss onlooker and parallel play – and in forthcoming chapters on thinking.

One example with a maraca egg

Joanne uses strategies that draw from intensive interaction (Nind & Hewett, 2001)[8] in order to 'slide in' and build rapport with Kyle, who is playing with a maraca egg. She adopts a role as a parallel player and uses 'mirroring' – being led by Kyle's positions and gestures as a useful way of generating a learning situation. She is able to develop communication and action learning with him.

Initially, she has to be careful about proximity and sharing his space. She plays alongside him with similar equipment and is succinct in her eye contact. She uses her own private commentary – audibly illustrating her thought processes – seemingly not directed at Kyle, but quite possibly providing him with incidental information or guidance.

Solitary play also has lifelong value

When we see solitary play on the developmental list, we might think it is only for children who have not yet developed social play. But even for the typically developing person who has good social skills, solitary play remains important throughout life. There are many ways in which we play alone, either consciously with a product in mind, like knitting, gardening or running, *or* less consciously, simply for the sensory process, such as handling things, fiddling or doodling. One interesting point about these processes is that they are people's thinking time; the actions are often internally accompanied by a reverie and are sometimes accompanied by self-commentary, which may be silent or muttered.

A positive aspect of solitary play is that it is individual time to learn and practise how to do things. Children can also develop concentration, persistence, self-reliance, etc., in solitary play. They will spend time refining sensory, perceptual, movement and manipulation skills through body play and object or action play.

Becoming more social

Moving on from the sensory and solitary beginnings, children typically use successive stepping stones. They become progressively more interested in observing and joining others. So, they begin to use 'onlooker' then 'parallel play', from which they gradually participate in 'associative play'. Being aware of these phases enables us to see progress and envisage strategies to illustrate information for them – or support the next steps in the development of their play. We can continue to use all of the strategies of sliding in and parallel dialogues discussed above.

Onlooker play

Observing without direct participation is common whilst children are in the early stages of developing vocabulary. You will often see younger children actively listening to the play conversations of older siblings or pausing to watch climbing or swinging techniques on playground equipment, and then possibly going and rehearsing these actions. It is an important strategy of absorption, and we should observe and recognise it in our special pupils, particularly some of those affected by autism.

With special children

If our pupils don't do this independently, we could promote opportunities for them to watch and learn. We can:

- Be aware of the value of them watching us, or peers, carry out everyday personal or practical tasks – which we can emphasise with our own commentary.

- Let them watch us engage in play of our own (e.g. sensory manipulations for exploration or pleasure or sequences of action such as stacking, packing, threading, modelling dough, etc.).

- Create opportunities, without pressure, for them to watch peers in practical or social activities or games.

- Let them see videos of themselves or their peers doing things.

- Subtly encourage them to respond to what they are watching with mimicking or commenting – using language or non-verbal strategies like showing and pointing or sign symbols.

Parallel play

With typical children, we see this a lot between the ages of two or three – they play adjacent to others, but not actually with them. They are aware of and do observe each other, and if you watch closely, you may see sidelong glances, elements of mimicry or the beginnings of synchronisation in their actions. This is a bridge between solitary and social play in which they observe patterns of how other people do things. Adults often enjoy parallel play as a way of being together (e.g. in pottery classes or parallel communication settings – conversations whilst driving in a car or whilst walking are often successful because the context can be more relaxed side by side).

With special children

Though it is easy to think of it as a transitional phase, parallel play has benefits in itself. For example:

- It provides contexts that reduce confrontation.

- It provides models of action and language.

- It enhances confidence about playing in proximity with others.

- It illustrates other people's intentions.

- It works towards initiating social interaction.

To promote parallel play, it is useful to have places around the classroom where it is natural to play or work alongside others (e.g. younger children may spend time in the home corner, sand tray or with construction toys, or older pupils may have social areas with magazines, books, music, games and arts and crafts), or garden and outdoor play areas are good for parallel experience. Working in parallel with adults on domestic chores or food preparation provides opportunities for parallel play and learning.

When pupils or students are engrossed in their own activities, adults may find opportunities for sliding in alongside them, using similar play or resources as indirect modelling and commentary to see if they can induce shared learning. A strategy as simple as sitting alongside students when we teach, rather than facing them, can make a world of difference.

 17.4 Online reading contains a parallel reading example

Associative play

Associative play is a step forward that happens through communication when children still play separately but become involved alongside others in what they do. For example, as they make their *own* Lego model houses, Sam and Dave may initiate some conversation by talking about their *own* ideas (e.g. "Mine's a car, it's got doors") *or* they may notice differences (e.g. "Your house ain't got doors").

Indeed, many adults enjoy contexts that offer associative experiences, such as pottery classes, knitting circles or gardening on the allotment. As you will know, joining a group requires opening gambits (e.g. if Otis wants to join the Lego game, he needs to use body language, shared looking, gestures, pointing or verbal statements and questions – something like, "Do you like my fire engine car, too?").

The ability to 'share attention' by making comparisons and having conversations about them enables typically developing children to turn parallel play into cooperation (Mundy & Newell, 2007).[9]

Barriers for special children

Our special children often get stuck on onlooker or parallel play. Researchers have suggested that this is because:

■ They lack verbal skills (opening gambits) to initiate or share interests necessary to associate themselves with groups (Beilinson & Olswang, 2003).[10]

■ Some autistic children lack spontaneous sharing skills such as showing things to others or pointing (Mundy, 2003).[11]

■ Penny Lacey (2009)[12] observed that many children with special needs are likely to accept situations rather make observations or comparisons. She suggested that they tend not to notice salient points in situations, express problems or describe preferences.

The barriers are about realisation and communication – sharing attention – and Lacey's suggestions were always about heightening pupils' reactions and awareness of making decisions by challenging them with real problems, such as there not being enough biscuits at snack time, and emphasising the need to:

■ Share attention

■ Initiate action

Her ideas fit well alongside all of the contexts of play in which a teacher can use various strategies, such arranging for things to be surprising or problematic, maintaining a commentary, etc. – all to provoke thinking. We can also arrange or teach opening gambits (e.g. whilst Otis is hovering, give him a really cool car to show to the others).

 17.5 See online material for an example of joining a hex bug game

Cooperative play

Usually, as the stages of play mature, typical children are able use all they have learned from integrating free play and socialisation in order to play cooperatively.

They understand having common goals and using rules and so they can fit into or even construct game scenarios, or enact and develop a narrative. These can also be rich veins of mathematical learning. But, as we have seen over the last few pages, the phases have difficulties for special children. All the works on special children's play that I have already referred to have suggested these children need help finding ways to grasp the structures of playing together. Nind and Hewett (2001)[13] have also suggested that supporting children in games and cooperative activities provides ways of teaching SLD pupils to play because they include:

- Joint activities – making mutual reference to shared meanings

- Repetition – reinforcing practice without boredom

- Alternation and turn taking – fundamental social sequences

- Creating motivation – positive attitudes to learning

- Creating problem solving – thinking skills without stress

It is important to recognise that, in playing games, children will learn from the processes as well as the content.

But should we limit our conception to practical social interaction? The inspirational teachers of literacy mentioned in online materials for Chapter 2 found ways to kindle imagination – why shouldn't our pupils experience the wonders and mysteries of the mathematical roots of life at their own levels and in their own ways?

Creative elements

Typically, as children enjoy playing both independently and collaboratively, they use a wide range of physical and social skills to explore many experiences, such as rough and tumble, competitive play, creative play, construction, arts and crafts, domestic play, social play, dramatic play, fantasy play, storytelling and more. In all of these contexts, children experience, manipulate and change things in shared play. Games are important, but there are also other ways of playing that we can participate in with our children in order to illustrate the world to them as best we can. There are many ways of playing, and our pupils should have the opportunity to access them – from sensory beginnings as far as our imagination can take theirs.

Imaginative play – special children and play partners

Vygotsky has written about the importance of children learning from interactions that involve make-believe play (1978)[14] *and also* about the importance of interactions with more capable partners in order to stimulate development (1976).[15] These two ideas point to how important it is that we should work on giving children experience of all kinds of play, including pretend play, imitation, reflection and make-believe through our own actions as imaginative play partners.

17.6 **See online reading for notes on reasons to be positive about imagination**

There are many ways of playing

All of the phases of playing often overlap as they develop and, in the mature player, they work together. When set into real contexts, they provide us with an endless variety of ways in which we can participate with children in ways that encourage them to play, and all of them always involve exercising mathematical learning.

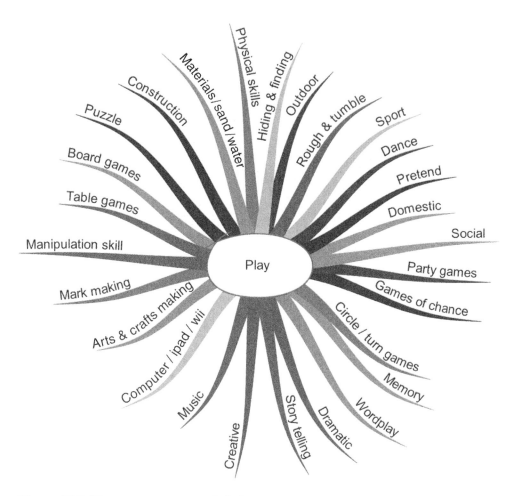

Figure 17.3 There are many ways of playing

Notes

1 Watson, D. & Corke, M. (2015) Supporting playfulness in learners with SLD/PMLD. In: P. Lacey et al. (Eds), *The Routledge Companion to Severe, Profound and Multiple Learning Difficulties* (pp. 365–374). London: Routledge.

2 Perry, B. D., Hogan, L. & Marlin, S. J. (2000) Curiosity, pleasure and play: a neurodevelopment perspective. HAAEYC advocate August 2000. Chicago: Childhood Trauma Academy, https://childtrauma.org/wp-content/uploads/2014/12/CuriosityPleasurePlay_Perry.pdf

3 Hewett, D., Firth, G., Bond, L. & Jackson, R. (2015) Intensive interaction developing fundamental and early communication skills. In: P. Lacey et al. (Eds), *The Routledge Companion to Severe, Profound and Multiple Learning Difficulties* (pp. 271–290). London: Routledge.

4 Caldwell, P. & Horwood, J. (2008) *Using Intensive Interaction and Sensory Integration: A Handbook for Those Who Support People with Severe Autistic Spectrum Disorder.* London: Jessica Kingsley, www.bing.com/videos/search?q=phoebe+caldwell+youtube& &view=detail&mid=AFB580D1EC0D6CDCE078AFB580D1EC0D6CDCE078&rvsmid=AF B580D1EC0D6CDCE078AFB580D1EC0D6CDCE078&FORM=VDFSRV&fsscr=0

5 I use 'join' in inverted commas because I want to emphasise the subtlety of *joining* the flow of their monologue and not superimposing adult directions, questions, etc.

6 Vygotsky, L. & Luria, A. R. (1929) The function and fate of egocentric speech. *Ninth International Congress of Psychology, Newhaven, Conneticut.*

7 Vygotsky, L. S. (1986) Thought and Language (A. Kozulin, Trans.). London: The MIT Press.

8 Nind, M. & Hewett, D. (2001) *A Practical Guide to Intensive Interaction.* Birmingham: BILD.

9 Mundy, P. & Newell, L. (2007) Attention, joint attention, and social cognition. *Current Directions in Psychological Science* 16(5), 269–274.

10 Beilinson, J. S. & Olswang, L. B. (2003) Facilitating peer group entry in kindergartners with impairments in social communication. *Language, Speech, and Hearing Services in Schools* 34, 154–166.

11 Mundy, P. (2003) The neural basis of social impairments in autism: the role of the dorsal medial-frontal cortex and anterior cingulate system. *Journal of Child Psychology & Psychiatry* 44, 793–809.

12 Lacey, P. (2009) Teaching thinking in SLD schools. *SLD Experience* 54, 19–24.

13 Nind, M. & Hewett, D. (2001) *A Practical Guide to Intensive Interaction* (pp 55–56). Kidderminster: BILD.

14 Vygotsky, L. (1978) Interaction between learning and development. In: M. Cole et al. (Eds), *Mind in Society: The Development of Higher Psychological Processes.* Cambridge MA: Harvard University Press.

15 Vygotsky, L. (1976) Play and its role in the mental development of the child. In: J. Bruner et al. (Eds), *Play: Its Role in Development and Evolution.* New York: Penguin.

Part 4
Thinking about thinking

18 About the development of thinking

From biological drives to communication and abstract thinking

As typical children widen their horizons beyond the personal exploration of their own bodies and immediate sensory environment, they become social learners. It is a journey in which they move on from being dependant on seeing or handling things to becoming able to hold mental representations in memory.[1] Such representations/memories are our first abstract ideas. As children hear and talk about their experiences, they are connecting them to the elementary language of maths. Starting to include words in their thinking gives them a tool for sharing comments and queries, which enables them to learn much more quickly and function effectively.

Typically, that learning spans the early primary years, but for children with learning difficulties, aspects of its development may begin later. It may even need encouragement to begin and support to continue, even into their adult lives.

There will always be debate about the extent to which very special pupils are able to use abstract thinking. My contention in this book is that abstract thinking begins with developing memory and visualisation – skills that *are* useful to the everyday lives of our special pupils.

Sensory and physical actions are thinking processes

Multisensory mental images

It is important to emphasise the multisensory nature of thinking because mental images are not just visual. They are from every sensory realm and include memories of movement, touch, etc., which all coordinate and trigger each other.

Schema again

As you read on into these chapters about ways that children start to develop mental representations, you will see connections to the patterns of physical activity – schema – which were described in Chapters 7 and 8 as being the roots of children's active thinking processes. The development of representations reflects schema in many ways – readers may find it useful to look back at the table in Chapter 8's online reading.

Circular motions make thoughts about circularity

My teaching assistant, Indira, has been watching Keera's mark making with chubby stumps. She is starting to show some interest in rotational movement, but doesn't complete a circle. Indira sits next to Keera with a piece of paper between them and starts to play herself. As she draws, she sings softly, "Round and roundy, round and roundy, round and roundy – round and round!" The song repeats, and Keera watches carefully as the circle is repeatedly drawn. She puts her hand on the back of Indira's and they hum together.

Later in the week, I see them outdoors, kicking leaves as they run around a tree. With each circle, they shout "Round again!" They are having so much fun that other kids join the game.

Phases of thinking

Thinking is a multi-layered process that passes through overlapping phases of development. It involves the biological roots that begin in 'core knowledge' (Chapter 4), and the physical beginnings of concrete thinking are seen in the actions of 'schema' (Chapter 8)

Jerome Bruner (1956)[2] described action-based learning with objects as 'enactive thinking' and he described how children's thinking progresses on from it. By making pictorial representations, 'pictorial and iconic thinking' is a step towards abstract thinking that can be connected to words.

Figure 18.1 gives an overview of the phases that children progress through, but I have included both developing 'visualisation' and using 'narrative thought' in it because these are both aspects of thinking that are usually taken for granted, but which special children need support to develop.

Whilst the phases develop sequentially, the earlier forms do not disappear.

Phases of developing thinking		
	Thinking at the beginning of learning	
Core knowledge	**Innate awareness** Infants have awareness of objects, persons, spatial relations. They even have intuitions that create expectations and affect their responses to events, these responses might be seen as their early forms of thought.	
Cause and effect	**Contingency awareness** As children become aware that their actions cause effects they deliberately use and repeat actions to see and refine – the memories and refinements seen in their actions are forms of thought.	
	Developing concrete thinking through action	
Developing schema	**Developing patterns of action** Children extend their cause and effect actions to explore and combine patterns of action which become formulas of responses.	
Enactive thinking	**Thinking with things** Initially thinking is *'concrete'* – without words. It begins with observing and acting on or arranging *real things*. Often children start to use showing objects and pointing as their means of expression.	
	Thinking adopts more abstraction	
Visualisation	**Using memories** Children start to use memories as forms of thought using ideas of object permanency. They can build upon the core knowledge of number sense which enables them to discern differences between small groups.	
Representational 'iconic thinking'	**Understanding images** Children can appreciate that images are depictions and understand that pictures, or the particular related sounds we make are acting as representations. They may have their own mental images (this is the beginning of imagination and visualisation). They make their own representations with their first words; and later with marks or drawing, which can carry 'iconic' or pictorial meanings.	
Using narrative	**Developing structure** Thinking develops as a sequential narrative. Being aware of the 'storyboard' creates structure and memorability.	
Abstract thinking	**Understanding symbols** Children generalise their understanding of imagery and appreciate that symbols can represent things – and ideas.	

Left margin: Phases overlap as they mature early phases continue to be used

Right margin (top to bottom): Beginning biological responses / Working through sensory / concrete actions / Remembering and representing

Figure 18.1 Phases of developing thinking

Understanding is a process of making connections between different kinds of thought

Another useful way of looking at the modes of experience that contribute to mathematical thinking is the triangular pyramid model (Fig. 18.2) presented by Haylock and Cockburn (2008),[3] who suggested that developing understanding entails making connections between the different ways of thinking. The pyramid illustrates how abstract thought is supported by other real experiences. The labeling of this version includes the use of pictures as well as other representations and visualisations.

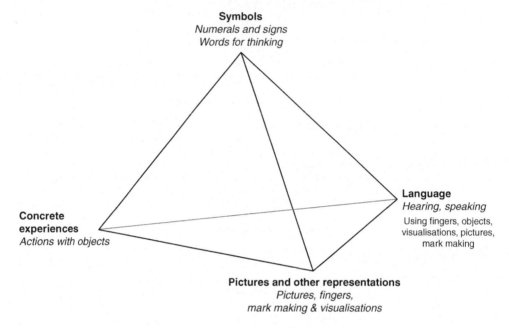

Children need to connect these aspects of maths to develop understanding

Symbols
Numerals and signs
Words for thinking

Language
Hearing, speaking
Using fingers, objects,
visualisations, pictures,
mark making

Concrete experiences
Actions with objects

Pictures and other representations
Pictures, fingers,
mark making & visualisations

Figure 18.2 Haylock and Cockburn's pyramid

Earlier on, Chapters 7 and 8 on physical skills and patterns of action described the beginnings of the processes of thinking schema. The chapters in this section will follow on from these and outline some of the factors that underpin the beginnings of mathematical thinking as a life skill.

Notes

1 They can see differences between small groups because of the perceptual 'number sense', which is part of the core knowledge they usually have at birth.
2 Bruner, J. S. (1956) *A Study of Thinking*. New York: Wiley.
3 Haylock, D. & Cockburn, A. D. (2008) *Understanding Mathematics for Young Children* (pp. 9–10) London: Sage.

19 | **Thinking with objects and fingers**

Enactive thinking with objects and actions

Initial sensory levels of play enable children to find out about the properties of objects, but as learning progresses, children use the objects themselves as props for thinking, and often watching and listening to what children do with them illustrates the ways in which they are thinking. This is perhaps most obvious when they use toys in social learning (e.g. one can easily see that play is reflecting thoughts when they play with dolls or play shopping). Working with special children, it is often useful for us to use such enactive play as an opportunity for modelling and commentary, and it can include a mathematical narrative (e.g. as things are added or taken from the shopping basket).

Thoughts about the nature of number are often being developed as objects and actions are used in practical activities or games. For example, when three balls are run down a tube into a box:

1. The child remembers the sequence of actions they made.

2. They collect the equivalent quantity of balls from the box.

3. They experience a particular name 'three' used by adults – or approved of if they use it themselves.

4. They may realise the connections between the action and language.

This, and others like it, is a process from which the abstract idea of 'threeness' will coalesce. But for a time, even typical children actually need the physical presence of the objects to know the number (Hughes, 1986).[1] During that time, there are many ways that children use objects in 'enactive thinking', making actions and arrangements that illustrate practical mathematical ideas. This time of concrete thinking is much longer for our special pupils. Consequently, we should participate with them in activities such as arranging items into lines and groups, comparing, building towers, connecting and separating, stacking and nesting or collecting and distributing. As we participate, we should maintain a flow of descriptive language –statements and questions.

Stacking and nesting

Stacking things that fit inside each other or making a tower illustrates a concept that children often find difficult (i.e. the idea that any large number actually contains all the numbers that come before it). Nesting them together is a way of illustrating that the last number counted represents all of them together.

Manipulatives – using things to think with

Many common things like pebbles, sticks, cups, bricks, bobbins, bead strings or fingers can be used as tokens that represent small numbers. Children naturally use them in many contexts such as outdoor play, sand play or domestic play or games. Using objects as tokens to tally events or scores within games makes them into representations connected to purposeful counting and to number value. Maintaining a narrative whilst using them encourages ordering of thought and memories, and this in turn provides a potential bridge to visualisation, Papert (1980)[2] called things that children can manipulate and arrange to *represent thoughts* 'objects to think with'.

Commercial manipulatives

There are many commercial manipulative products such as Cuisenaire, Numicon, etc., they not only illustrate small numbers but also the structure of the number system. Research confirms that using visual and manipulative equipment is beneficial for many with learning disabilities (National Education Association, 2002),[3] and approaches to teaching like '*Maths Recovery*' that set out to promote number sense all incorporate visual and manipulative equipment.

 19.1 The online reading goes into much more detail about the use of manipulatives and provides further references

Virtual manipulatives and apps

There is now a growing range of virtual manipulatives that put the images on screen. Cuisenaire environment[4] or Numicon whiteboard resources are examples. These resources have value particularly for those pupils who engage well with screens, and they are also good for sharing group work, including children acting as demonstrators. But, after all I have written about the power of touch and movement, my view has to be that whilst they are valuable supplements, they are not a complete substitute for original tactile objects. Depending on the app, it is often possible to devise physical resources that can be used alongside them. One commercially available number app for young children that has its own manipulatives is Tiggly Maths.

Starting to game

The block-building game Minecraft has PC and iOS versions that have proven to have the capability to engage and are being used in schools around the world, drawing children into designing forms and environments. There is even a dedicated education version.[5] David Isaac, a teacher at Sir Charles Parsons School, is an enthusiast who suggests there are many objectives in the game that are suitable for more able special pupils, particularly relating to three-dimensional space and multiplication. Isaac noted that when the games were initially set up for lunchtime clubs, some students struggled to maintain respectful cooperative styles of play and were intent on killing each other in the game, burning houses, etc., but more recently, these same students have become extremely good colleagues during the playing of the game and they have now developed several social skills that they previously lacked.

In some cases, simple Minecraft constructions created on a PC or tablet could be replicated in Lego or on a large scale with cardboard boxes to provide a tactile or kinaesthetic three-dimensional experience that could be of value for some pupils. There are other, simpler commercial 'play' apps that are inexpensive, including a range of Lego construction apps with themes ranging from Duplo to Star Wars that can be equated to real constructions, as well as a Lego movie app with which you can create single-frame animation movies of what you are making with real bricks as you build it.

Apps for number activities

Apps of games like 'Paper Toss' or 'Can Knockdown' give positive experiences of turn taking and provide opportunities to track sequential activities and scoring and to make comparisons. But it is also good to involve pupils in real versions of these games and use real manipulatives for recording, tracking and keeping score.

A special place for fingers in mathematical thinking

Most people recognise the potential for a connection between fingers and learning to count, but the depth of their connection to our mathematical brain is not fully exploited by mainstream curriculum thinking – here is some food for thought.

Fingers and their connection to core knowledge

In Chapter 4, discussing the sensory beginnings of maths, I outlined how children are born with core knowledge, upon which they build learning, and that includes a 'number sense' (Spelke & Kinzler, 2007)[6] that enables them to *perceive differences* between small groups of up to three or four items. This is the first process of discrimination that forms the basis of later numerical thinking. Neuroscience has shown that these perceptual processes happen in the left parietal lobe, which, in addition to this perceptual function, also controls finger manipulation.

The perspective on fingers and counting

It seems certain that, historically, finger counting preceded counting with special words, and linguists tell us that the origins of number names are actually rooted in the words for fingers and hands. Both Butterworth (1999)[7] and Dehaene (1999)[8] in separate books discuss these relationships and suggest:

i. Over millennia, fingers have played a role in the development of counting.
ii. Counting on the fingers is still an integral part of the processes children use to develop and extend the mental number line[9] – on which we all represent quantities.

It is certainly true that if we observe typical infants and children as they are developing their numeracy skills, they spend hours manipulating their fingers and looking at configurations and combination of fingers while muttering number words. During these processes, they begin to remember and understand the relationships of numerosities in terms of the visual and tactile sensations of finger patterns. They do all this naturally, and mathematics curricula contain little reference to finger counting, despite the connections found in neurological research that suggest fingers have a role as the first symbols of quantity.

The purposes for which children use their fingers in counting seem to be common to all cultures. For example:

■ Finger pointing itemises and denotes the individuality of one item.

■ A sequence of pointing actions can define a group that can then be named.

■ Children match fingers to sets of real things.

■ Using sequential pointing works towards a number line.

■ As fingers are used to count, they become symbols – they are representations of the things that have been counted (Hughes, 1986).[10]

■ Children naturally keep tally with fingers – they provide a useful visual and tactile aid to memory.

- Fingers are used as calculating tools in representing the parts of simple arithmetic problems, being manipulated (e.g. raising fingers for addition and folding them for subtraction).

- When children use fingers instead of itemising real objects, they are taking a step towards abstract thinking.

About fingers and special children

Whilst finger manipulations are too easily regarded as simple sensory motor learning, neuroscience is now telling us that the natural inclination to use fingers as representations is actually the beginning of symbolic representation and thinking, so manipulation skills and symbolic thinking are intertwined. Children who seem unaware of these processes or those who are unable to manipulate their own fingers are disadvantaged by being deprived of experiencing sensations that usually underpin understanding quantity and sequence. It may be helpful for them if teachers use touch as a communication medium as they count, so that the children are provided with tactile/spatial signals about quantity and sequence at the same time as they are offered visual or auditory numerical information, symbols or language. There will be more about fingers in later chapters about number sense and counting.

Some examples of hand and finger work

These activities might be used *alongside modelling speech* in a wide range of contexts

- Hand massage and shared finger play

- Handling items, particularly with textures, bumps or holes

- Developing independent finger fascination and play

- Developing pincer grip

- Arranging small items

- Developing finger pointing as a communication strategy

- Coordinating reaching and touching with sequential sound making

- Single-finger pointing to one object for itemisation

- Alternating finger pointing to a second object

- Sequential pointing at the items of groups

- Pointing along a line of things sequentially

- Finger shape and sequence games

- Matching finger representations to sets of objects

- Using finger shapes to show or demonstrate size

- Using fingers to track or communicate about sequence

- Using finger shapes as representations – realising they are a form of symbolic representation

- Using finger shapes to help hold things in memory

- Realising fingers can be used as a calculator

  - Tracking sequential increase

  - Counting

  - Combining hand groups

  - Folding back

All of these can be incorporated or modelled in practical or social activities and games, and many will reoccur as root skills within the principles of counting.

Examples of resources

- Toys with sequential holes, bubble wrap, strings of beads, balls and Numicon

- Tiny toys or sorting buttons for sequential touching

- Finger dabbing artwork

- All sorts of gloves for accentuating and sharing attention to fingers

  - Including sticky spots on the end

  - Lighting white or fluorescent gloves with a single LED ultraviolet keyring light

- Using biscuit or modelling dough with Numicon shapes or children's modelling material

- Using rings or hair bobbles on their fingers as representations

Notes

1 Hughes, M. (1986) *Children and Number*. Oxford: Blackwell.
2 Papert, S. (1980) *Mindstorms*. Scranton: Basic Books.
3 National Education Association (2002) Instructional materials survey: report of findings. In: *Research on the Benefits of Manipulatives*, www.learningresources.com/text/pdf/Mathresearch.pdf
4 Cuisenaire environment, https://nrich.maths.org/4348&part=note
5 Minecraft Edu, http://services.minecraftedu.com/wiki/What_is_MinecraftEdu
6 Spelke, E. S. & Kinzler, K. D. (2007) Core knowledge. *Developmental Science* 10(1), 89–96.
7 Butterworth, B. (1999) *What Counts* (pp. 195–226). New York: The Free Press.
8 Dehaene, S. (1999) *The Number Sense* (pp. 92–95). London: Penguin.
9 It is an interesting point that the cultural history of the development of counting actually reflects the natural learning processes still used by children.
10 Hughes, M. (1986) *Children and Number*. Oxford: Blackwell.

Visualisation – using all senses

Mental images

In *How the Mind Works*, Steven Pinker (1999)[1] explains that all our experiences become represented in our minds as mental images. Sometimes we can see them as in dreams; other times they are subconscious. It has become accepted that '*visualisation*' can be used as a form of thought in many aspects of life; for example, it is used therapeutically to change emotional reactions or in sports to improve physical performance. Later, we will see that visualisation plays a role in the development of ideas about number. Our mental images are not just visual – they occur in all sensory dimensions as patterned memories and can be associated, compared, sequenced and combined to make new ideas. Though teachers and parents informally do lots of things – particularly with infants – that promote these sensory memories, the conventional curriculum doesn't emphasise the need to deliberately teach children to use mental images. However, an awareness of how non-verbal imagery develops might be useful to us in teaching special children to think.

Developing visualisation

The very beginning

Right at their roots, cognitive development and the development of number begin with many simple interactions. There is much that we can highlight in our children's practical lives and games that seems simple but is vital to cognitive development – including understanding number – even starting with cause and effect.

Peek-a-boo, memory and anticipation

In typical development, infants' facial recognition is a rapidly developing indication of their visual memory, as is observed in children when they focus on objects after a break and show recognition.[2] It may seem like humble beginnings, but Bruner (1976)[3] emphasised the import role of 'peek-a-boo' interactions to the beginnings of cognitive development. Some of our special children still need exercise in developing these fundamental understandings, and this includes remembering sound patterns and actions.

To exercise and develop skills related to connecting memory and consequences for older pupils, we need to recognise where such interactions involving memory, anticipation and surprise occur in older lives. 'Peek-a-boo' has the same elements as a magic trick – 'now you see it, now you don't' – which has plenty of fascination for adults. It has also been described as one of the fundamental structures of all good jokes. It involves surprise balanced with expectation (Stafford, 2014),[4] and we can find it in many aspects of everyday experiences, particularly in games. It also occurs with movement in dancing and, of course, in song.

Object permanence

When we observe a child seeking something that they believe should be there, we know that they are using an appreciation that objects are permanent things, which is a foundation block of cognitive development in understanding the world (and number).

As Bruner observed with peek-a-boo, the appreciation of *object permanence* develops from natural human interactions usually seen between infants and carers, such as developing eye contact, sharing attention to objects, following eye gaze and tracking movement,[5] particularly tracking things and seeing them disappear and reappear (Routes for Learning, 2006).[6] Developing object awareness occurs in all sensory modes, such as feeling for hidden objects in bags or moving to find things that have disappeared behind the furniture or locating an animal you can hear in the long grass.[7] These may seem like fundamental levels, but the principles underlie many activities that promote the development of visualisation even for more mature pupils – or adults.

Visualisation is a form of thinking

Using the mental memories of objects and movement is a fundamental part of practical thinking. As I have noted above, such memories are initially exercised within interpersonal reactions like peek-a-boo or shared attention and develop into games of hiding and revealing or seeking and finding with infants.

Such experiences promote the use of short-term memory by mental imaging and widen the appreciation and application of object permanence. In later chapters, we will come across the roles of mental representations – using all senses – as forms of visualisation that make up the number sense. We will see how they become part of abstracted thinking, how they are used for making comparisons and, through subitising, are part of the processes of learning about numbers.

We can promote visualisation in many practical activities and games that involve recall, searching and hiding, revealing and finding, putting things in boxes, drawers or bags, etc., remembering where things have been left or are stored, noticing if they have changed, etc.

Visualisation activities can also be reinforced by using pictorial representations, such as using pictorial lists, or taking photographs to use during recall sessions. Objects hidden in a game can be recorded using picture cards that are matched up to them as they are found. Children also like to watch videos of themselves and activities they have participated in – some examples are in the text box.

Ways of exercising visualisation/memory

Games

What's in the bag? Or where have the biscuits gone? Matching card games, Find the lady, Kim's game or treasure hunts. Games involving hiding, anticipation and revealing using boxes, tubes, drawers, bags, etc., temporarily hide items to play memory games or guessing estimating contents – when the contents are revealed, they can be recorded and rechecked.

Practical

Exercising memory of storage locations of possessions, food or utensils in the kitchen, checking shopping bags, storing shopping.

Memory activities exercise thinking and frequently connect to mathematical aspects of knowledge such as identifying or comparing small quantities by looking, sequences and classification.

Visualisation and number

In later chapters, we will find out how comparing visualisations of objects to the mental number line is an important facet of children's early ability to think about the notions of 'increase' and 'decrease' and bridge from practical addition and subtraction to later numeric processes.

Experiments carried out by McCrink and Wynn (2004)[8] with a puppet theatre showed that very young infants were able to predict the outcomes of adding or taking away one or two puppets behind a screen, which suggests that they are capable not only of holding images from events in their mind, but also of deducing expectations of arithmetical outcomes from memory of what they had seen. They have a visual sense of quantity long before they can count.

The puppet theatre experiment was also adapted by Jill Porter (2005),[9] who explored the abilities of SLD children to visualise and identify small numerosities. She suggests that whilst Down syndrome children are delayed, many do progress and catch up (though this is not *necessarily* the case with all other conditions). She suggested that it could be useful for teachers use 'hiding and revealing' activities to teach children to practice visualisation of quantities.[10]

The work of Martin Hughes (1986)[11] showed that many preschool children can add and subtract small numbers even if the objects cannot be seen, so long as the problems are set in language that they can visualise. For example:

a) The children could answer an imaginary problem such as, "If you have two sweets and I give you two more, how many will there be?"
b) But they were unable to answer the question, "What is two and two?" because they can't envisage the quantities in it.

The findings of all these researchers offer us some useful thoughts for good teaching:

- Initially use motivating contexts – with real things.

- Encourage children to visualise by using hiding and revealing.

- Be aware of the maze of word difficulties.

Think back to the previous chapter and all that was said about promoting thinking by using real things or manipulatives – visualising is stepping towards abstract thought. It runs in parallel with all that will be said in the next chapter on making marks and all that will be said later about number sense.

Notes

1 Pinker, S. (1999) *How the Mind Works.* New York: Oxford University Press.
2 Much of the early research on number sense – such as the puppet theatre experiments and the looking time test – that we will discuss in later chapters were also based on observations of infants' ability to remember what they had been looking at.
3 Bruner, J. S. & Sherwood, V. (1976) Peek-a-boo and the learning of rule structures. In: J. Bruner, A. Jolly & K. Sylva (Eds), *Play: Its Role in Development and Evolution* (pp. 277–287). Middlesex: Penguin.
4 Stafford, T. (2014) 'Why all babies love peekaboo', BBC, www.bbc.com/future/story/20140417-why-all-babies-love-peekaboo
5 All of which are fundamental skills that some PLD and autistic children need support to develop.
6 Routes for Learning (2006) Additional guidance, Appendix 5. Cardiff: Welsh Assembly, www.complexneeds.org.uk/modules/Module-2.1-Planning-to-meet-needs/All/downloads/m05p080b/routes_for_learning_additional_guidance.pdf
7 Routes for Learning (2006) provides a flow diagram of the development of object permanence for sighted learners.

8 McCrink, K. & Wynn, K. (2004) Large number addition and subtraction by 9 month old infants. *Psychological Science* 15(11), 776–781.

9 Porter, J. (2005) Assessing awareness and coding of numerosity in children with severe learning difficulties: three exploratory case studies. *British Journal of Learning Disabilities* 33(1), 1–5.

10 Some of her suggestions for using hiding and revealing include creating situations where number has practical meaning, using game approaches and using small sets of consistent objects.

11 Hughes, M. (1986) *Children and Number.* Oxford: Blackwell.

21 Thinking using marks and graphic representations

Long before they use numerals, typical children use other kinds of representations to 'read' or record representations of quantities. The processes they use include understanding the pictures or icons they see and making their own marks and pictures. These are simple beginnings and are close to concrete activity, but nonetheless are important forms of representational thinking. They bridge towards more abstract forms of thought. stay useful to us throughout our lives – we all use pictures, marks and icons.

Understanding representation role of pictures

Typical children may recognise people and things in pictures when they are as young as three months old (Barrera & Maurer, 1981),[1] but findings suggest that early on they tend to think of pictures as '*objects of action to use*', rather than '*images for thinking about*'. For example, children may sometimes try to put their feet into a picture of shoes or try to put their doll into the image of a bed (Penner, 1991).[2] Even into their second year, many are still refining the idea that they can use pictures for generalised communication and representations (Deloach et al., 1994).[3] This suggests that we should not underestimate the need or the value of teaching our special children about various uses of pictures, such as:

- Shared looking – illustrating that meanings in pictures can be shared

- Using them for learning about remembering and naming

- Using pictures for communication – for asking and telling – *a precursor to icons and symbols*

- Using them as labels – for representing and organising things

- Planning – arranging pictures in order to anticipate how events will happen

- Using pictures to record and retell what happened

Many of these activities can include using pictures alongside the real things in games, for functional purposes such as labels for hidden or stored things or for mathematical purposes, representing sequences or quantities.

Making marks

Typical infants enjoy the processes of mark making, and the sensory feedback that it gives them motivates practice, which develops motor skills. However, in addition to manipulation skills, as described in Chapters 7 and 8, the physical movement also generates forms of thinking (schema).

The early years publication *Mark Making Matters* (DCSF, 2008)[4] emphasises that, for typical children, stages of 'scribbling' are analogous to the role babbling plays in learning to talk.

> When children realise that marks can be used symbolically to carry meaning, in much the same way as the spoken word, they begin to use marks as tools to make their thinking visible.

It is true that:

▪ Even before their graphics are clear, we can often detect emergent mathematical thinking in children's rhythmic actions when sequences of marks correspond to quantities of things or events.

▪ As graphics become clearer, children often talk to themselves about quantities or events as they are drawing.

Making marks, making meaning

In their book *Children's Mathematics*, which is poignantly subtitled *Making Marks, Making Meaning*, Worthington and Carruthers (2003)[5] describe the typical progression of children's thinking through mark-making phases, which include:

I. Early sensory mark making

II. Developing schematic action and representation

III. Making pictorial depictions

IV. Using pictorial narrative for reasoning

Sensory mark making

Worthington and Caruthers suggest that when infants make movements to make marks, this shows they are interested in deliberately affecting the world around them. Even before they hold implements, typical children are fascinated by the kinaesthetic pleasure of making marks by playing with food, sand, foam, mud, etc.

There are observable phases of development, but they also overlap. At times, children show interest in different patterns of action, such as banging or horizontal, vertical or circular movements, which are all explored and the schema for which are gradually refined. Through this process, they learn about the space in front of them and practice actions such as banging and linear and circular movements. As their hand grasp improves, children can use implements or markers.

All of this is relevant to children developing understanding about deliberate action and communication. It is also a good opportunity for teachers to participate and model language related to aspects of quantity, position and meaning that occur in their actions and drawings.

This development is not easy for our very special children. They often have poor manipulation skill that prevent the development of fluent drawing or writing.

Those children who have profound physical difficulties may need us to support them or find alternative experiences. Participating in movement or arts and crafts experiences together provides such opportunities. New technologies, including tablet apps and eye gaze drawing, are opening up exciting possibilities.

 21.1 Online reading contains a discussion about aspects of mark making for very special children – and examples of art activities

Schematic level

As sensory mark making refines children's control of linear and circular actions and develops other patterns, actions emerge such as 'dabbing' and 'enclosing'. A description of some schema that relate to mathematical thinking was outlined in the online reading for Chapter 8 (Table 8.1) when I discussed 'schema' and how 'physical skills' develop into thinking.

Some examples that develop and combine might include:

- Banging actions gradually refining to more controlled dabbing, which may eventually synchronise to become capabilities such as making one-to-one marks or marks in lines or groups.

- Drawing lines becoming deliberately vertical or horizontal.

  - Following lines develops awareness of direction, sequence and connecting things.

  - Combining vertical/horizontal movements makes squares or grids.

- Circular scribbling refining into drawing circles.

  - Children recognise these as enclosures that can contain things.

  - Children develop the idea of making marks inside boundaries, which leads to defining sets.

Alternatives to drawing

When children have difficulties with drawing, we have to see if it is possible to find alternatives, such as using craft activities like printing or stickers – sometimes using ideas that spring from using objects such as printing in dough or using building bricks or other objects.

One way of compensating for poor drawing skills is to make representations by using objects, such as placing items onto paper plates or using fridge magnets on trays.

One class had great lessons making their own Minions using eye stickers. They invented a new Minion and called him Freddie Three Eye. The teacher took pictures and made a book on the iPad with an app called Book Creator.

 21.2 An example of how one schema develops into useful actions – dabbing

Pictorial level

When children are able to draw enclosures, control dabbing and make marks inside boundaries, their mark making may take on pictorial elements to which they may assign meaning and show awareness of representing quantities (e.g. they may call a shape they have drawn 'a house' and the marks within it windows or people).

With special pupils, we may need to work on pictorial representations by providing images, for example, pictures that can be taken from books, magazines or catalogues and either printed on paper or used in drawing apps.

Narrative level

Typical children and some of our special children use pictorial representations as forms of reasoning, such as drawing and talking about the real things that are aspects of a maths story. In one example in the online reading, Joseph draws marks he calls dogs next to houses and can work out how many dogs live in his street.

This may be a high level for many of our special children, but it refers back to using pictures, and again, it is something that we could do with either paper cutouts or using storyboards and drawing apps.

 21.3 Online reading about using pictorial representations and reasoning

Using tokens and tally marks

As icons to represent groups

When typical children are aware of using the one-to-one principle in the process of counting, they consolidate the connection with finger matching. They also develop the use of recording by either collecting one token or making one mark per item to represent a group. Butterworth (1999)[6] tells us that such development in children actually reflects the pre-historical development of counting, which first used tally marking[7] for representation. Following the use of fingers, scoring, marks on sticks or collecting tokens all predate written numerals and the abacus. Though it has ancient beginnings, tally marking is still commonly used, even by adults, to keep track of ongoing events or keep score.[8] In an online example, Alfie makes iconic line marks alongside his picture to represent the apples he has drawn on the plate.

There also seems to be a natural affinity between using objects such as counters as tallies and icons and making marks as representations. We can exploit that affinity when we use games for teaching purposes – by incorporating both giving tokens for scoring and then making marks to record the score. Doing this we both reinforce the different ways of making representation and create repeated modelling. For example:

1. Get the child to lay their counters in a line (the teacher says how many there are as if thinking aloud - *using private speech*).

2. Then both count together to check.

3. Then draw around each one.

4. Then take them away and count the circles again.

Done with panache, this can be made a fun part of the game – but the purpose is reinforcement because it generates a lot of repeated modelling.

Many teachers use Numicon shapes informally as tokens in games for scoring – or as part of manipulation activities, such as by drawing around them, printing with them by using paint or pressing into dough or placing items into the corresponding holes.

Dice, playing cards and spot cards

Using iconic marks is a precursor to using spot cards, dice or playing cards. Games can be created that use only cards or dice with only small numbers. We will return to spot cards and ten frames, which can be used for scoring in games when we discuss number sense and subitising.

Notes

1 Barrera, M. E. & Maurer, D. (1981) Recognition of mother's photographed face by the three-month-old infant. *Child Development* 52, 714–716.

2 Perner, J. (1991) *Understanding the Representational Mind.* Cambridge, MA: MIT Press.

3 DeLoache, J. S. & Burns, N. M. (1994) Early understanding of the representational function of pictures. *Cognition* 52(2), 83–110.

4 DCSF (2011) *Mark Making Matters.* National Archives. Nottinghham: DCSF publications, www.foundationyears.org.uk/files/2011/10/Mark_Marking_Matters.pdf

5 Worthington, M. & Carruthers, E. (2003) *Children's Mathematics: Making Marks, Making Meaning.* London: SAGE.

6 Butterworth, B. (1999) *What Counts* (pp. 197–225). New York: The Free Press.

7 The word 'tally' is derived from the Latin *talea*, which means 'cut twig' or 'stave'.

8 The word 'score' also means to make a mark.

22 Using numerals – a medium for abstract thinking

Having the sense of size

It seems to most of us that mathematicians who can think with enormous numbers work in an abstract ether by understanding patterns of higher thinking, but at first even they have a sense of the sizes represented by the symbols.

Most of us have of a grasp of the quantity that a small numeral represents – if we see a number '9', we have a quick sense about how much this represents. That's the beauty and usefulness of numerals – they help us overcome the limitations of our perceptions. We actually grasp the size quicker than if we had been shown nine things or tally marks, which we would have had to count. Seeing a numeral or hearing its name, we can also compare it to other small quantities to make immediate decisions, because we have a sense of their sizes. Adults who can use symbolic decoding (e.g. in reading words) can actually use numerals as part of their number sense. They can even make approximate comparisons of large numbers. There are confident mathematicans who are fluent in seeing large numerals and grasping their size.

But many of us start to lose touch with exact comprehension of numerals, either when the groups they represent get beyond our perception or imagination or when there are too many noughts in the numeral to see easily.

Number sense, subitising and numerals

I will talk about number sense and numeral identification more in the chapters on number sense and particularly Chapter 33 on subitising. Initially, children's thinking about number is dependent on perceptions of real things. They learn to apply names to groups of things they look at, which is 'perceptual subitising'. Later, they associate the names with numerals and can envisage the groups just by hearing the name or seeing the numeral – this is called 'symbolic subitising'.

Ideas that are needed

The fact that numerals are symbols that represent particular quantities is some-thing that early learners are absorbing before school. They soon start talking as if they know what they mean, but in reality, understanding takes time, and we will see in later chapters that they need lots of practice in making estimations.

Some of our special pupils who are starting to appreciate graphic representations need experiences that link numerals to both quantity and the purposes they can be used for. When we are modelling and working with such pupils, we need to ensure:

▪ The numerals we use relate to quantities they can conceive of.

▪ They encounter practical uses of numerals; for example, to record a quantity they need to remember, to take a message, to use in a shopping list, to record a score or to translate a picture.

About numerals and numbers

Are numerals numbers?

We often take it for granted that numerals *are* numbers, when actually they are notational symbols – representations of numbers – but not the whole idea!

Many typical two-year-olds can name some numerals, but this does not mean that they associate the image or word with its actual quantity. The writing of numeral shapes is usually described in the curriculum around children's fourth and fifth years. But children's understanding will not be complete unless they appreciate all of the following connections:

▪ A numeral is a symbol that is associated with an individual number word.

▪ The same words are used for counting.

▪ Each word stands for a quantity.

They also need to have a sense of the comparisons between the quantities the symbols represent.

The link between the ideas of '*number*', '*numeral*' and '*quantity*' is easily taken for granted. In reality, this link takes some time to coalesce through experience. So it is important that when we write numbers with children, we should do it in a context with meaning, so the children can really experience the connections (i.e. see that numerals represent size and are arranged in order).

When children have very special needs

The majority of special children that this book describes are cognitively delayed, and many do not become fluent like their peers at symbolic levels. Amongst our special pupils, there are various levels of understanding. Some children are predominantly at sensory levels, some concrete, and some are beginning to become numerate. For most of them, these levels overlap.

Sensory learners

Sensory or physical barriers constrain pupils with profound difficulties from fully relating to the use of graphic numerals, but this does that mean that we should not expose them to cultural encounters with numbers and numerals that occur in social interactions, games and practical activities, where they occur continuously. Being part of a duo or group that shares looking and reacting to pictures or symbols that have numeric content is part of learning about 'shared meaning'. It is the mathematical equivalent to sharing books with very young children. We don't hesitate to share books with children long before they can actually read words because we know it provides all sorts of background learning. So long as we do not have unrealistic expectations, there is a great deal of benefit from using number words and numerals within activities and games – they promote awareness of communication and sharing information about quantities and sequences. If we create motivating circumstances, they may also generate a child's interests at levels we may have previously underestimated.[1]

Concrete learners

A majority of our pupils in special schools are concrete learners for whom experiences with *real things* are still the most relevant aspects of learning. Most of these children are not fluent at counting, and when either counting or numeral recognition is being modelled for them, we need to be very aware of including experiences that:

1. *Develop their perceptual number sense, including the ability to subitise* (i.e. look and say the number of a group without counting). In games, social events or practical activities, our modelling should include making immediate estimations of small groups (*subitising*) and showing numerals.
2. *Raise their awareness of the purposes of using numerals* by ensuring the children encounter them being used as labels for real things or to tally and record immediate events. Our modelling should illustrate ways of using numerals in practical activities or games:

   ▪ Alongside counting, ordering and positioning of objects

   ▪ Alongside tracking sequences or turns

   ▪ As labels for quantity – matching to groups and labelling them

   ▪ For comparison of value – bigger or smaller

   ▪ For memory recording – making lists

Visualising, subitising and counting work together

In later chapters, you will find a description about how *'perceptual number sense'* develops into *'subitising'*:

1. Perceptual subitising – at first, children name small groups of objects or visual patterns.

2. Symbolic subitising – this occurs later, when they can visualise group size just from seeing numerals.

Children's ability to think abstractly about number has to mature through coordinating *both* the processes of subitising and counting.

Concrete learners with some graphic awareness

As some pupils develop fluency in counting small groups, they may develop consciousness of graphic numbers as labels and for counting. Opportunities for extending their awareness occur during practical activities, games or social events. We can introduce the use of numeral cards alongside the real objects used in the game or on price tickets, continually drip-feeding number recognition and naming into the flow of activities.[2] For example:

- Making a pictorial shopping list provides an opportunity to use graphic numbers meaningfully alongside pictures of items.

- Participating in a game like 'Smack the Number' (with a fly swatter), 'Magnetic Fishing' or 'Number Snap' all provide opportunities to model naming numerals, as well as the opportunity to pay out the quantity with tokens or coins.

There are many more examples of games that can use scoring or numeral recognition on Pinterest and on iPad or tablet apps.

 22.1 See online reading for more about working with concrete learners who develop some use of graphic awareness

Pupils with numeric performance

There are a few pupils, particularly amongst those on the autism spectrum, who can carry out calculations purely using numerals, but it is *also* true that some get correct answers without really understanding the quantities involved or appreciating what the answer means practically.

Even though they have apparent skills with symbolic number, such pupils still need to develop connections to reality through experience of practical handling of real things and representations with manipulatives. Much of the work on number sense and many of the resources described in later chapters are also relevant to helping these pupils. Developing their sense of comparisons between larger numbers is one important issue. Approximation activities such as estimating the numbers of sweets in different jars or making comparisons between different large groups and representing them with large numeral cards (e.g. "That's about 20 – but that's 50") would be good experience. Printing tickets for a show – for the class or for the whole school – would be another. One amusing book on this matter is called *How Many Jelly Beans*.[3]

 22.2 See online reading for more about working with pupils who have some numeric performance

Possible confusions with numbers and numerals

For all of the groups mentioned above, one key issue we too often underestimate is – do children understand what numbers are for?

Difficulties occur because we use numbers in lots of different ways (e.g. sometimes they are for exact practical purposes and others times for fun in games and songs). Complications also arise because, even in the simplest processes of counting, the number names are used with different meanings:

- *As ordinal numbers*

  - In a sequence to show order

- *As cardinal numbers*

  - To end the counting sequence *and* name the size of the group

Adding to the confusion, sometimes numbers are just used as nominals (e.g. the number shown on a Number 55 bus is a name – it's code for its route, it's not the 55th bus to pass that day). The kind of misconceptions described in the following text box are common, so when we are modelling, we need to be conscious of making sure the purposes of our counting or labelling are explicit.

Some examples of ways that numerals can be confusing

The number on Thomas the Tank Engine is always a 1, Gordon is 4 and Henry is 3, but if you place them on the track, neither the order you placed them in or the quantity of engines on the track necessarily matches the numerals that are on the engines.

As another example, count a row of children and give each a numeral card. When you call the last one 'four', he may naturally think that's *his* number. He may not understand that you may be using the word to describe the whole set.

There are a myriad of other confusing examples. One teacher told me that she had difficulty explaining that 'blast off!' was not a number.

Perceptual difficulties

Even in normal development, discriminations such as between 2 and 5, 6 and 9, 6 and 0, 14 and 41, etc., take some time to develop. Researchers suggest that the processes of refinement are not only related to visual skills, but also are associated with auditory processing and motor skills (Brooks et al., 2011).[4] In typical development, children usually overcome these problems, but with our special pupils, we need to be aware that misperceptions may also be compounded by neural processing difficulties. They may see reversals or numbers moving on the page due to difficulties with contrast or glare. These issues were previously discussed in Chapter 14 on perception.

Writing numerals

Very few of the pupils to whom this book relates are fluent in drawing or letter formation. Even the most able benefit from motivational multisensory practice activities exercising not only mark making but also other fine manipulation and spatial skills *and* exercising short-term memory. For example, arts and crafts, playing with tiny toys, making matchbox collections, winding threads, making string or elastic band patterns, making and baking number shapes with dough and writing in foam or sand or even in the air are valuable for all. For suggestions that focus directly on numeral writing, return again to the Down's Syndrome Association's writing download.[5] There are also numerous apps that support numeral recognition and finger manipulation, including 'Dexteria' for general dexterity or 'Writing Wizard' for letter formation, both of which feature on the Seashell Trust's blog entry '14 apps to develop literacy skills'.[6]

There many ideas on Pinterest that have Montessori roots like tracing, textured shapes, sand or other tactile materials. Recent years have seen many developments, like the verbal and rhythmic activities of Dough Disco. One abiding rule is such approaches should be motivating.

 22.3 See online reading for more about written reversals

Notes

1 It is entirely possible that the advent of eye gaze software may literally open up our eyes as to what some students really know.
2 It is also useful to make use of manipulatives as forms of illustration, as discussed in the previous chapter.
3 Menotti, A. & Labat, Y. (2012) *How Many Jelly Beans*. San Francisco: Chronicle Books.

4 Brooks, A. D., Berninger, V. W. & Abbott, R. D. (2011) Letter naming and letter writing reversals in children with dyslexia: momentary inefficiency in the phonological and orthographic loops of working memory. *Developmental Neuropsychology* 36(7), 847–868.

5 Down's Syndrome Society. Education support packs – writing, www.downs-syndrome. org.uk/download-package/primary-support-pack/

6 Seashell Trust (2016) 14 apps to develop literacy skills, www.seashelltrust.org.uk/blog/ 14-apps-develop-literacy-skills

23 Language, thinking and memory

In the previous chapters, I have discussed ways of thinking with objects or visualisations that occur without spoken language. Though we are not conscious of them as being thought processes, they are important elements of our thinking. When they occur, they often prompt us to talk, so language and non-verbal forms of thinking intertwine. Verbalising our non-verbal thoughts is another process of thinking, and when we do it, our ideas are refined in a more conscious way.

The way we use language matters

Children with SLD have delayed language development and do and not use verbal thinking to the same extent as their typical peers, and this tends to change the way we interact with them, in particular:

- There is a tendency for adults to organise things for SLD pupils and, as a consequence, the children exercise less experience of independent thinking about the need to solve problems.

- Whilst organising and caring for children, adults tend to use more language that directs or commands their actions, rather than language that refers to ideas or requires children to explore and respond with observations or comments (Buium et al., 1974; Marshall et al., 1973).[1]

These tendencies reduce children's awareness of problem solving and independent action. Different approaches are needed in order to provoke children to think and encourage them to be interested in affecting changes to quantities, space and time and develop thinking skills that apply to life maths.

Creating problems to think about, talk about and solve

Penny Lacey's prescription for encouraging SLD children to engage more in using thinking skills was to make the curriculum connect to real living (Lacey, 2009).[2]

She suggested that teachers should use the organisation of everyday practical and social situations, particularly working on children's short-term memory power, including within games and play. The essence of her ideas is that situations should be arranged to present problems that children can respond to and resolve. She included:

- Modelling verbal thinking, including maintaining a stream of consciousness commentary as guiding talk to emphasise points of attention.

- Using language *about* thinking to lead children into awareness of problem solving (e.g. "Oh, I thought there was enough – what's wrong? What do you think?").

- Even using mischievous sabotage as a strategy to provoke children into responding.

23.1 Online reading includes an example of provoking thinking in a game

The online reading example describes a game in a lesson where participants win Hula Hoops crisps by rolling a dice. The teacher provokes children's responses and thinking by inadvertent miscounting – actually blatant cheating – whilst playing a game.

Penny Lacey's suggestions have been liberally expanded upon by Imray and Hinchcliffe (2014)[3] in their chapter on problem solving and thinking, where they particularly advocate for using the real contexts of practical activities and games *and* creating circumstances where pupils are taken outside the comfort zone of routines.

Thinking aloud

In Chapter 17, when thinking about solitary and parallel play, I discussed some aspects of private speech and suggested that, whilst teaching, we should consider using commentary as a guiding speech strategy, depicting our own thoughts or projecting a narrative of possible action to provide information and prompt children's thoughts in an indirect fashion.

Giving ourselves instructions

Self-talk can also be useful for memory. Even adults often talk to themselves to guide their own actions through tasks; in fact, it is a common strategy of police advanced driving or pilot cockpit drills. It can be a useful strategy to teach some children to help themselves stay on task (Alderson-Day & Fernyhough, 2015).[4]

Researchers have found that the use of self-regulatory speech is linked with better problem solving (Fernyhough & Fradley, 2005; Winsler & Naglieri, 2003).[5]

Enhancing memory skills

Using recall and rehearsal are processes that strengthen working memory and enhance possibilities of immediate retention, promoting links to longer-term storage, which improves the chances of connecting and modifying ideas.

Rehearsal and repetition

We all use rehearsal; for example, when there is a new phone number to remember, we may repeat it back to ourselves aloud to keep it active in memory until there is a chance to write it down.

Research also suggests young children with low working memory capacity may benefit from being encouraged to voice or repeat key information (Müller et al., 2009).[6] So it makes sense to use this approach in our own commentary and encourage children to use verbal rehearsal.[7] Though rote learning is often spoken of critically, it has a culturally proven place. The construction of memory songs and verses provides a powerful key, particularly for learning sequences, and such songs can be used to connect and reinforce other understanding.

Recall

Adults often use the process of going back through the narrative of actions to trigger recall and reinforce learning (see below).

Thinking about thinking

In contrast to the tendencies mentioned earlier about how we often use directive rather than descriptive language with our pupils, Penny Lacey (2009)[8] often made the point that we should try to use talk that makes children *consciously aware of their own thinking*. She suggests that our responses and questions should include 'mental verbs' and phrases like "What do you *think/know*?" "Can you *guess/ remember*?" "Have you *forgotten*?" "What do you *mean*?" as well as other '*thinking*' words such as 'if', 'because', 'why', 'what' and 'when'. Including such words creates situations where children can be prompted to be conscious of thinking – as Penny puts it, 'conscious of mental events' – and gives them experience of hearing and seeing thinking routines in action (Salmon, 2008)[9]. To her view I would add that the emphasis, intonation and even body language that we use with these enquiries can be key influences in drawing children's attention to the idea that there is something that they need to think about and tell us.

Using a narrative is a thinking process

Making and listening to stories have fundamental roles in the way we think. Bruner (1991)[10] noted: "We organize our experience and our memory of human happenings mainly in the form of narrative."

Making a narrative is often used as a process to remember things. For example, if you have lost your keys, you go back sequentially in your mind through all the things you have done since you last had them. Exercising narrative is an element of developing memory, but it has other uses; for example, we tell people things – even justify our actions – by relating all of the steps of events that happened to us. Or narrative from the past can be a basis of anticipating what the future could be; for example, we describe what happened last time we went to the shops in order to plan our next visit.

When we make a narrative, we juggle and connect the parts of our observations to make what we think is the best pathway for our story (Bruner, 1991).[11]

It is a form of reasoning – the processes of 'telling' and 'thinking' are intertwined: *telling the story is thinking*.

Narrative thinking has relevance in mathematical thinking. The problem-solving process is itself the unfolding of the sequential story of: (1) finding out; (2) doing; and (3) outcomes.

Using 'narrative' to provide context and structure for special children

The scaffolding of a story can help special children recall events, express the sequences of actions and be led to think about responses and outcomes. But with special children who think at concrete levels, it is important to support thinking by using real things and pictures to accompany verbal narratives or instruction. Research indicates that short-term memory difficulties hinder the verbal understanding of many SLD children, who have comparably better visual memory (Wishart, 1998)[12] and remember better if they have observed and actively touched things.

The value of using narratives to teach begins before numerate levels

In literacy, it is generally accepted that storytelling teaches children skills even before they can read. These skills are also relevant to developing thinking and fundamental mathematical learning because stories provides many circumstances in which to use guiding talk to model mathematical language, illustrating the use of numbers and processes that make things change.

Stories include opportunities for:

- *Sharing looking and listening* – thinking together about changing elements of quantity, space and time. A great deal of learning to think happens through joint attention. It might be part of following sequences of events, developing anticipation of what is next and thinking about what the consequences might be. All of these involve observing and are background to expressing responses.

■ *Participating* – just like other stories, maths stories can be organised to include action or enacting together in participation – with real things.

■ *Retelling* – repetition and retelling by either the original teller or other participants helps develop memory, promotes fluency and embeds and reinforces learning. When retelling, children are also given the opportunity to introduce different perspectives, think about adaptations and other applications or step on to next levels.

■ *Application* – embedding knowledge from the story into responses.

■ *Adapting* – learners recognise similarities and differences in everyday situations and are encouraged to select the best responses – to do it the same or to do it differently – either reinforcing or adapting their established ideas.

■ *Creating* – new responses develop from new situations or reacting to unusual events (e.g. 'what if?' events created by staff).

The narratives of practical activities

Practical and social activities provide ideal contexts for using narratives for learning because within them there is always a cycle of awareness, planning, action, outcomes and review, which is ripe for recording and sharing. There can be different approaches to developing and communicating about events that are relevant for different children. Scenarios can be factual or enacted – adding unexpected elements generates alternative thinking, fun and problem solving.

 23.2 See online reading for more about using narratives of practical activities using representations in narratives

Typical children will often retell verbally, but with special children it is useful to have other means of representation to support stories. Objects of reference – photos from the event, other pictures or symbol cards – are all alternatives that can act as bridges connecting the real objects or events to memory, thought and planning.

Such alternative representations can be useful alongside verbal discussion or directions in each phase of activity.[13] They can be used in various ways, such as:

■ For planning – pupils are involved in selecting objects, pictures or symbols from a pack and arranging them to anticipate events.

■ Using them as action prompts during the processes of doing.

- Using them as checklists (e.g. matching the pictures to the items bought).

- Making representations for retelling (e.g. setting out objects or pictures in the order of the story).

- Prompting the child's own verbal comments – objects and pictures stimulate opportunities for discussion.

- Using fingers as a means of tracking and representing the sequence.

Recording narratives

Stories including practical events can be recorded and used for retelling:

- Collections of objects and pictures (some could be collected into a story box).

- Watching video clips.

- Photographs made into a book.

- Photos taken on a phone or tablet will be in order – as the camera roll is scrolled through, memories of sequences are prompted.

- The camera pictures can be made into e-books with storyboard apps that can be printed or used on-screen.

Notes

1 Buium, N., Rynders, J. & Turnure, J. (1974) Early maternal linguistic environment of normal and Down's syndrome children. *American Journal of Mental Deficiency* 79, 52–58; Marshall, M., Hegrenes, J. & Goldstein, S. (1973) Verbal interactions, mothers and retarded and non retarded children. *American Journal of Mental Deficiency* 77, 415–419.
2 Lacey, P. (2009) Teaching thinking in SLD schools. *SLD Experience* 54, 19–24.
3 Imray, P. & Hinchclffe, V. (2014) *Curricula for Teaching Children and Young People with Severe or Profound and Multiple Learning Difficulties* (pp. 204–208). London: Routledge.
4 Alderson-Day, B. & Fernyhough, C. (2015) Inner speech: development, cognitive functions, phenomenology, and neurobiology. *Psychological Bulletin* 141(5), 931–965.
5 Fernyhough, C. & Fradley, E. (2005) Private speech on an executive task: relations with task difficulty and task performance. *Cognitive Development* 20, 103–120; Winsler, A. & Naglieri, J. (2003) Overt and covert verbal problem-solving strategies: developmental trends in use, awareness, and relations with task performance in children aged 5 to 17. *Child Development* 74, 659–678.
6 Müller, U., Jacques, S., Brocki, K. & Zelazo, P. D. (2009) The executive functions of language in preschool children. In: A. Winsler, C. Fernyhough & I. Montero (Eds), *Private Speech, Executive Functioning, and the Development of Verbal Self-Regulation* (pp. 53–68). Cambridge, UK: Cambridge University Press.

7 In fact, it was also found that when children's self-regulatory speech was suppressed (e.g. they were told to work silently), problem-solving performance was adversely affected because they could not plan ahead; Lidstone, J. S., Meins, E. & Fernyhough, C. (2010) The roles of private speech and inner speech in planning during middle childhood: evidence from a dual task paradigm. *Journal of Experimental Child Psychology* 107(4), 438–451.

8 Lacey, P. (2009) Teaching thinking in SLD schools. *SLD Experience* 54, 19–24.

9 Salmon, A. (2008) Promoting a culture of thinking in the young child, *Early Childhood Education Journal* 35, 457–461.

10 Bruner, J. (1991) The narrative construction of reality. *Critical Enquiry* 18, 4.

11 Bruner, J. (1991) The narrative construction of reality. *Critical Enquiry* 18, 4.

12 Wishart, J. (1998) Cognitive development in young children with Down syndrome: developmental strengths, developmental weaknesses, www.riverbendds.org/index. htm?page=wishart.html

13 Decisions about the nature of representations – objects, pictures, icons, symbols, etc. – will depend upon the needs of different students, sometimes using different representations (e.g. objects plus symbols can be useful).

Part 5
Developing mathematical ideas

24 Introducing aspects of mathematical thinking

There are some very fundamental elements

So far, this book has looked at the roots of thinking and learning for mathematics. As it has related to the tools and processes of learning, it has touched on many general aspects of learning. In the chapters to come, I will take the focus closer to look at some of the important precursors to mathematical thinking that grow from these tools and processes. I will start with sensory awareness of objects, which is relevant for all pupils, but particularly those at the earliest levels of learning. Then I will progress through understanding of size, quantities, sequence and value, and head towards counting, symbolic representation and thinking about number, which some of our special pupils come to use.

I will refer to studies of how typical children develop their understanding of number because, like Dr Jill Porter (2015),[1] I believe that the messages about number sense are relevant to us knowing about the development of our special pupils.

 24.1 See online reading on Dr Jill Porter and roots of number

All the areas I introduce below are dealt with in more detail in the following chapters.

Developing mathematical thinking

Sensory learning – about objects and space

Fundamental awareness of objects
Early levels of 'object awareness' are not usually specifically associated with the 'mathematics' curriculum, but nevertheless part of the root of mathematics is understanding the nature of objects. Even the most fundamental idea of 'object permanence' is an important foundation.

Awareness of groups

Considering sensory exploration of objects and space is important because we need to know how children perceive that objects are associated together into groups and how that is affected by spatial arrangements. Appreciation of space and understanding number are intrinsically intertwined. We will see later that how the brain has constructed mathematical thinking is itself related to spatial perception.

Understanding sequences

Ideas related to order grow from memory of sequential sensory actions. They develop alongside practical and social experiences such as processes of collecting and distributing before they are connected to quantities and numbers.

Understanding time

In recent years, neuroscientists have become interested in the relationships between children's intuitive sense of interval timing and the development of numerical abilities. A theory of magnitude (Walsh, 2003)[2] proposes that the development of ideas about time, number sense and space all share common cognitive roots. It is suggested they all evolve from sensory experiences that focus on 'more' or less than/greater than. Allman et al. (2012)[3] review the literature in relation to both typically developing children and groups with neurodevelopmental disabilities.

Understanding sizes

Children's development of fundamental ideas about size begins with sensory learning, including manipulation and movement, which evolve into making choices and comparisons. But developing thought beyond concrete levels depends upon associating their experiences with language. Initially, the language of size evolves from social experiences – hearing people talk as they participate in using things. Later, the language of physical size has to be generalised to relate to also describing quantities.

The beginnings of numeric learning

Number sense – perceptions of quantity

An idea that I first introduced in the chapter on aspects of perception is that we are born with an intuitive 'number sense' and are able to perceive differences between small quantities even at birth. Elizabeth Spelke[4] and others believe that this is part of the core knowledge from which all subsequent mathematical understanding is built. Research expanding on the ideas of core knowledge is highlighting the role of perception in learning about number, and with the growing awareness of dyscalculia, there is interest in those developments even as they apply to mainstream pupils.

Subitising

Later, there is a chapter on how the intuitive number senses merge into 'subitising' groups – which is the immediate perception and naming of small quantities. It is both a useful life skill and essential, alongside counting, for learning to think about number. In fact, in some of the coming chapters, we will find that these perceptual skills remain important, as even educated adults use them as tools in their mental mathematics (Dehaene, 1997).[5]

Typically developing children and adults progress from perceptual subitising to symbolic subitising – when thinking can be triggered by using numerals. Only a minority our special pupils become fluent at that level.

Fundamental ideas about quantity

Number sense is instrumental in helping children develop a fund of early ideas about quantities. Even before their use of number names is mature, they are developing awareness of:

■ Making comparisons

■ Increase and decrease

■ Parts and wholes

These are important ideas for practical skills even before children use number, but as the ideas are connected with language, children begin to be able to communicate first of all about general ideas of quantity and comparison and later to associate them with numbers.

Counting

As the idea of 'number' – *that particular quantities have names and can be ordered according to size* – evolves, so does the practice of counting. It is through counting that children extend their understanding and move beyond the limitations of the intuitive number sense.

This is a period of learning that the conventional curriculum tends to see as *the* beginning point of mathematics. It also tends to assume that counting is a straightforward development, because for most children it seems to be a naturally developing skill. Conventional curriculums tend to require practicing it as a *whole* and don't focus on either:

■ The influence of number sense

■ The detail of the sub-skills that children need to use to be able to count

In the chapter on counting, I will outline those sub-skills that I might call 'the parts of counting' in more detail because many children with special needs struggle with them. We will see that the conventional curriculum is starting to recognise the importance of number sense.

24.2 See online reading for why we should use counting with children who may not master its skills

Some 'big ideas'

Many mathematicians have recognised that the fundamental ideas about quantity that evolve in children's minds about 'size', 'order', 'time intervals', 'how things change', etc., usually coalesce to form a set of 'big ideas' about what 'numbers' are about and how they work. They start with the one-to-one principle and include the idea of a number line and understanding about value or magnitude. In the chapter on big ideas, I will explore some of these that are particularly relevant for our special children not only because they are important parts of knowing about number, but also because they are important to the *practical* understanding and application of ideas that are important life skills.

Notes

1 Porter, J. (2015) Using number in everyday life. In: P. Lacey et al. (Eds), *The Routledge Companion to Severe, Profound, and Complex Learning Difficulties* (p. 316). London: Routledge.

2 Walsh, V. (2003) A theory of magnitude: common cortical metrics of time, space and quantity. *Trends in Cognitive Science* 7, 483–488.

3 Allman, M. J., Pelphrey, K. A. & Meck, W. (2012) Developmental neuroscience of time and number: implications for autism and other neurodevelopmental disabilities. *Frontiers of Integrative Neuroscience* 6, 7.

4 Spelke, E. S. & Kinzler, K. D. (2007) Core knowledge. *Developmental Science* 10(1), 89–96.

5 Dehaene, S. (1997) *The Number Sense: How the Mind Creates Mathematics*. London: Penguin.

25 Some sensory beginnings of number

Awareness of objects, groups and sequences

In Chapters 4 and 14, I described some of the starting points of mathematical knowledge we have at birth. That '*core knowledge*' provides the expectations from which we begin our explorations.

Object awareness

In Chapter 14, I noted two aspects of core knowledge that are particularly relevant to the beginnings of mathematical learning. For pupils with very special needs, they were 'object awareness' and 'number sense'. In straightforward parlance, these might be described as providing:

- Awareness of things
- Awareness of groups of things

To those we could add:

- Awareness of magnitude drawn from senses of time and space

These aspects of core knowledge are precursors to all mathematical thinking, which spring from being aware of the space and time around us and the things in it. Just as natural understanding of the shapes and properties of things in space has to develop a long time before we can think of that knowledge as 'geometry'. Similarly, before you can know anything about 'number' or 'counting', you need to be aware that 'things' exist alongside each other, appreciate they can become grouped or sequenced and how they are arranged and rearranged in space and so on. Such levels of thought may not be included in the conventional curriculum, but they are the deep foundations. We have to think about teaching these foundations, which are aspects of object, temporal and spatial perception, to many of our very special pupils, but particularly those with profound difficulties.

This chapter, and those immediately following it, explore some of the fundamental learning that underpins learning about number. It includes:

■ Developing working memory and understanding object permanence

■ Tracking and understanding sequential movement

■ Awareness of spatial arrangement and groupings

■ Experience of sizes and comparisons

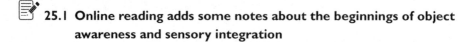 **25.1 Online reading adds some notes about the beginnings of object awareness and sensory integration**

Object permanence

Understanding that things continue to exist when they are out of sight and cannot be seen, touched or heard would rarely be listed as a mathematical idea in the conventional sense. But being able to envisage and think about things when they are not present is in fact a root for abstract thinking.

Initially, this skill develops from experiences of objects being encountered alongside experience of cause and effect. It is particularly stimulated through watching other people do things.

For children, the realisation of *object permanence* is an essential part of carrying out practical activities that reach beyond the immediate moment. It is a factor in their transition from purely object-related thinking to being able to anticipate or plan beyond immediate experience. It is also a forerunner to both visualisation and using representations – not only those such as pictures, but also, in the longer term, symbols, including numbers.

The natural development of object permanence

To develop object permanence, the child must carry a memory of visual or other sensory images, such as sounds or touch, which can prompt them to seek or search. Early developmental behaviours such as hiding or throwing and retrieving contribute to its development, and as typical children practice them, their experiences of cause and effect develop and they refine their powers of anticipation, intentional action and planning.

Awareness of object permanence develops through a range of levels at different periods in children's cognitive growth. Typical children initially develop their appreciation through progressive personal, social, practical and playful experiences, such as:

■ Returning and seeking glances

- Experiences of touching and being touched – developing body sense and spatial awareness

- Peek-a-boo[1]

- Experiences of having and discarding items

- Experiences of tracking items and seeing them disappear and reappear

- Remembering returning objects

- Experiences of going to different places – and returning

- Locating things in their usual place

We may need to provide these experiences, exercising multisensory searching at various levels and in contexts like practical or social activities as well as games, modelling them through our own participation in age-appropriate ways.

The missing lipstick

Dawn likes make-up, so we have lipsticks, nail varnishes and some nice tins she can sort them into. There were five lipsticks that fitted exactly in a row in the tin. One morning when she had been using them with Fiona, her teaching assistant, during break time, I took two lipsticks out and hid them at the back of her drawer to see if she would notice they were missing. After break, when they got the tin out again, Dawn was alarmed and a search ensued. There was a lot of opportunity for mathematical communication.

 25.2 Online reading includes a longer list of suggested activities for exercising understanding of object permanence

Awareness of movement, spatial arrangement and groups

Examples of activities throughout the book include experiences of moving and arranging, hiding and revealing objects, which obviously contribute to the practice of physical skills that are important for independent life. We discussed '*schema*' in Chapter 8 – remembered patterns of action – that are the first forms of thinking and practicing activities, such as placing things in order, stacking/nesting, collecting items together into containers, various kinds of mark making, etc., which all contribute to mathematical ideas. *You may wish to return to Chapter 8 for the fuller description – I will discuss this more in coming chapters when I discuss 'understanding size and comparisons' and the processes of counting.*

Movement and spatial distribution

Many of the examples of activities described above and in the online reading throughout the book include experiences of spatial relationships, sequences and grouping. Even at birth, typical children are interested in linear tracking of moving things and sounds. Through that innate interest they develop experiences of linear space as well as expectations about the behaviour of objects (Welsh Assembly, 2006).[2] For example, typical children expect a ball that disappears behind a screen to reappear, and this suggests they have the basis of an idea about object permanence that can be developed. Anyone who has rolled a ball down a tube with a toddler, even one who is less than a year old, will know they have a fascination for movement and reappearance in a different place that soon becomes an expectation. Other aspects of games like that (e.g. the sequential repetition of actions and placement of objects in lines or in groups) are also fascinations that introduce mathematical concepts such as appreciating order and sequence, which themselves are at the roots of counting and understanding about value.

Perception of groups

In Chapter 14 about perception, I mentioned the processes of 'perceptual constancy' – how children come to recognise objects from different angles or as they move partly or fully out of view – and 'perceptual grouping' as factors affecting children's identification of groups. Some of the activities I have listed and the way you handle and arrange things in games could be used to exercise children's group perception with the aim of enhancing their capacity to observe changes. But there are some natural, biological limitations that point to the value of providing our children with practice. Attention is limited to a small number of objects at a time – even adults can generally only attend to three or four moving objects simultaneously. These limitations influence the earliest levels of information gathering, and though most people develop strategies to accommodate them, those difficulties are certainly the root of issues for some pupils, so it is well worth finding ways to practice intuitive responses to size. Indeed, rapid identification or comparison of groups – developing 'number sense' – is increasingly being identified as a key to progress for many pupils who have difficulties with number, including mainstream children with dyscalculia. These issues will be discussed in later chapters on number sense.

Notes

1 Bruner (1976) recognised peek-a-boo as an interactive foundation of cognitive development (see Chapter 20); Bruner, J. S. & Sherwood, V. (1976) Peek-a-boo and the learning of rule structures. In: J. Bruner, A. Jolly & K. Sylva (Eds), *Play: Its Role in Development and Evolution* (pp. 277–287). Middlesex: Penguin.

2 Routes for Learning outlines the role of tracking moving objects in developing object permanence for pupils with profound disabilities. It quotes Kiernan's description of how object permanence begins and develops through children's sensory coordination of tracking. See Routes for Learning (2006) *Additional Guidance.* Appendix 5. Cardiff: Welsh Assembly, which draws from Kiernan. C. (1981) *Analysis of Programmes for Teaching.* Basingstoke: Globe Education.

26 Comprehending space, shape and measures

Understanding the physical world

Typically developing children progress quickly through learning to explore their physical environment and the things in it. They absorb language so quickly that by nursery age the conventional curriculum focuses on teaching them the language of naming shapes in preparation for formal geometric language. Our special curriculum needs to focus on developing their sensory and practical understanding of their environment and useful communication.

The emphasis may be on:

- Sensory and practical understanding of the space around them

- The practicality or pleasure of shapes and sizes

- Experiences of magnitude – weight, volume and forces

- Experience of time

But we will find that experiences of all these things are also at the roots of understanding about number and value. *There is even a chapter in this book called 'Number is like space'.*

Throughout the book, I have spent time talking about spatial perception and understanding the nature of objects. Readers may refer back to discussions about children's processes of discovery through touch and movement in Chapter 12 and the processes of developing ideas from action illustrated in Chapters 7 and 8. Those chapters on physical and sensory exploration encapsulate the essence of the space, shape and measures curriculum for very special children. The mind map in Fig. 26.1 illustrates the kinds of practical life skills and knowledge that are relevant to learning about the geometry of life and measures for living for very special children or adults.

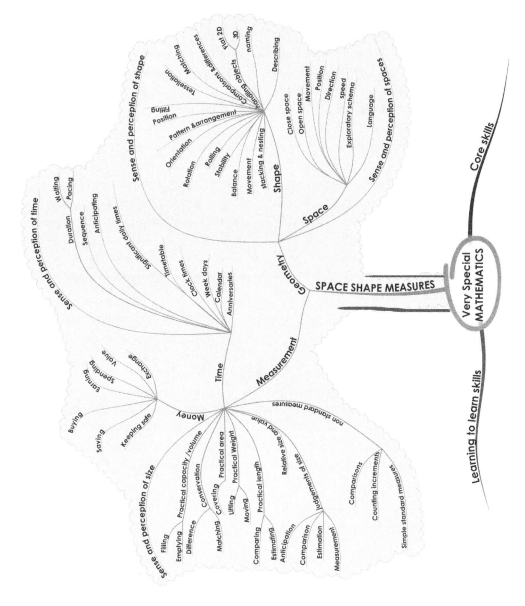

Figure 26.1 space shape and measures

Shape and space – the geometry of life

Understanding the geometry of their environment starts from the core knowledge that infants usually have at birth. It first includes some awareness of their orientation and perception of close space. They develop it though looking, reaching, touching and moving. As they focus their sensory attentions on the boundaries of shapes and the contrast of edges and planes, they start to build spatial maps and object appreciation. They continue all this in wider contexts when they reach and become capable of handling things, learn to move around and know about spaces and places. In every kind of activity, they build ideas through the schematic patterns of actions that I have described. Of course, children with sensory and physical difficulties are hindered in these processes – some of them profoundly.

Developing practical understanding and responding to practical words of shape and position are more important for our pupils than knowing lists of geometrical names. The priorities for them are developing appreciation of the nature of objects, positions and spaces. Our aims, across all levels of performance, must be to enable them to respond, use things purposefully and improve how they can express observations and preferences.

 26.1 Online reading includes notes about the development of language about the real world

Sensory levels

For everybody, but particularly those with PLD, learning begins at sensory levels, perhaps as simply as experiencing open or confined spaces and learning to observe, handle and place objects. There is so much to learn – for everyone – from practicing manipulation and movement and hearing people talk about the world, thereby learning about names, actions and consequences. For some of our pupils, connecting this sensory level to language and action remains at the heart of their curricular needs.

Concrete levels

Most children will progress to activities to satisfy their daily needs. They apply their practical perceptions and growing knowledge in processes of matching, sorting, placing, etc., which all reflect practical thinking. They learn in all practical contexts where ideas about shape and size are used (e.g. they may learn about the directness of 'straight' by following a line or throwing things, or the recurrence of a circle by going around in a circle or playing circle games). They enjoy exploring and learning to apply action ideas like 'covering' and 'containing', the stackability of boxes or the various uses of rolling. As they enjoy experiences like these, some may appreciate or use common language, such as 'round' or 'straight' or descriptions of position.

Abstract thinkers

A few may reach the level of being able to visualise and talk about things or draw them. Some may use common or even geometrical language for abstract talk and thinking about things (e.g. thinking about whether an object will balance, fall over or roll away, why something won't fit, whether to use a round or square cake tin, etc.).

For all our special pupils, there are many things to learn about the practical geometry of life and a range of levels for participation and teaching.

 26.2 Online reading includes some activities for working on space and shape and measures for living

Measures for living

Measuring depends upon understanding about size. Even before we can use numbers, as infants we measure by comparison and estimation, and we keep on doing so for the rest of our lives. In all its incarnations – distance, capacity, weight and duration – physical size matters a lot to us – it can be motivating or disappointing. Understanding physical size is related to understanding quantity.

Children's actions are the first forms of communication that show us they are making choices about size. The language of 'again', 'more' and 'all gone' is early to develop and that tells us how important it is.

Sensory levels

All pupils, but particularly PLD pupils, will need to develop skills of observation and exploration as they encounter objects and materials of different sizes, weights, etc., and as they experience time, including events of different durations or speeds. In working with them, we should aim for them to develop an awareness of change and the power they have to cause change.

Concrete levels

Most pupils can participate in practical activities and games and experience the need to make choices by using comparisons. They may learn from hands-on trial and error such as matching and fitting and develop practical responses regarding consequences in activities that involve weight, volume, quantity, etc. They may appreciate the use of pictorial timetables, anticipate events and learn about waiting.

In games and practical activities, they may show interest in managing changes of sizes and respond to or use some everyday words of size comparison, like 'bigger' or 'more'. They may appreciate some of the ways that measures become related to number (e.g. gaining or losing, winning, receiving more, receiving less or exchanging or paying for things).

Abstract thinkers

As they anticipate changes or think about the consequences of differences they have observed, a few pupils may be able to comment on comparisons or differences of size and value using everyday language. They can be aware of problems and talk about solving them, which may include understanding comparative values or relative costs and the use of money. A few may be able to relate to some more specific mathematical language.

 26.3 Online reading includes some more experiences related to roots of measuring for living

Connections with number

Concepts of physical size and concepts about quantity are interrelated. In later chapters, we will find that spatial perception is one of the key elements required for developing 'number sense'. Neuroscientists point out that brain areas that are active when thinking about quantity overlap and interact with areas involved in spatial judgements. They even suggest that our existing brain circuitry for number has evolved from areas that were previously dedicated to spatial perception (Dehaene, 2010).[1] In fact, it is now well established that intuitive decisions such as seeing which plate has the most biscuits or which playing card has more hearts all arise first from spatial perception. It is also true that many words we use for describing physical size are also used for describing number.

Some of our special children will need support to develop both spatial perception and language about physical size and number.

Note

1 Dehaene, S. (2010) The calculating Brain. In: D.A. Souza (Ed.) *Mind Brain and Education*. Bloomington: Solution Tree Press.

27 Learning about size and comparisons

We use comparisons in order to make choices – but it is also true that we learn about making comparisons through making choices. Choosing is an important form of thinking and it often revolves around judgements of size and quantity.

Making comparisons

Making comparisons is fundamental for practical living. We use it for making choices when we notice differences. Our minds slip into mathematical mode as we naturally want to know about the difference or to tell or ask someone about it (e.g. "You've got more than me!").

Before they can express themselves about numeric quantities, children must understand general ideas about the sizes of physical things. The previous chapter noted that the roots of numeracy are connected to understanding about space, shapes and measures, but there are also connections in the language that is used.

Thinking about physical comparisons

Pioneers of early years education like Froebel and Montessori recognised that children's ideas about size develop through playful physical experiences. The roots of comparisons and reasoning begin as children use their perceptions and explorations as tools for seeing differences and making choices. With typically developing children, we take the thinking processes involved in choice making for granted, because it develops in the general flow of life and doesn't seem to need much specific teaching. But as Penny Lacey and others suggest,[1] many special pupils need us to teach them about problem solving. We need to encourage them to react with curiosity, examine things and be aware of looking for differences – learning to make choices and communicate about them.

For children at different levels, this will include:

At sensory levels

■ Reacting to stimuli and learning to make contingent responses.

■ Developing awareness of cause and effect.

■ Extending that awareness into deliberate action.

■ Learning to share attention.

■ Experiencing people making decisions – acting on them and talking about them.

 27.1 Online reading describes an example of rock sorting play with Tyrone

Concrete and social levels

■ Sharing deliberate action and handling things together.

■ Learning to observe and look for differences.

■ Using matching and sorting.

■ Making deliberate choices – with awareness of reasons.

Beginning to use practical reasoning

■ Noticing the consequences of similarities and differences.

■ Expressing differences.

■ Learning about refining decisions and changing things.[2]

■ Learning about communicating about differences – asking and telling.

Processes of observation

Using physical manipulation as a process of observation is beneficial to all our pupils, but it is particularly important for children at sensory levels. Physical skills like reaching, handling (even mouthing), banging and placing things are all forms of action *thinking*, and as they become more intentional, they open up opportunities for choice making and making concrete comparisons.

With some of our pupils who are at very early levels of learning, we need to develop their awareness of looking for differences – perhaps even the physical activities of observation and directing attention. Valuable work can be done with sensory resources. It may be useful for practitioners to be aware of the interplay of different movements and kinds of actions that they could encourage, some are described in this online reading.

 27.2 Online reading gives a more detailed description about making comparisons – starting for very early learners

Processes of discrimination – pairing, matching, sorting and ordering

The observation and exploration skills I have described support the development of pairing, matching and sorting things, which are important because they give children awareness of thinking about how things can be the *same* or *different* and an opportunity to articulate reasons. There are many opportunities to work on and model these in play, with puzzles or with practical activities such as sorting cutlery and crockery away, sorting clothing, etc. Sorting things by physical size has particular connections to later mathematical learning – not least because much of the same language used in doing this with 'things' will later be applied to describing numeric quantities.

The language of size and comparisons

Absorbing general words about size

Children's exposure to language starts long before they have vocal language. It is present in their earliest experiences of social cause and effect.[3] Even in early feeding sessions, babies experience their parent's non-verbal behaviour and commentary about quantity and sequence, and babies make responses that show they are developing anticipation about quantities. As language develops they learn via generalisations, for example, it is interesting to note that during the one-word phase of development, children often use 'again' as a word for 'more'. To an extent, the words are carrying similar meaning. This reinforces the idea that we need to maintain modelling of action and these words – and the words that expand them, at even the most fundamental levels of communication.

As typical children's social, practical and exploratory worlds expand, their responses motivate adults to provide more sophisticated language models. As typical children differentiate and absorb the nuances of language such as 'big' or 'bigger', 'small' or 'smaller' and 'more' or 'less', their experience of language and ideas about comparing sizes evolves. For most children, this is a process of natural absorption, but it cannot be taken for granted with children whose language development is falling behind. Teachers of special children must accentuate modelling to enable children to appreciate the functions of words that describe size.

Relating the language of size to groups

So far, the focus has been mostly on how children learn to describe and compare the physical sizes things. But there is more, because as typical children absorb the language of physical size, they also encounter the ways that adults use similar *and sometimes even the same* words to refer to *groups of things.* So gradually children begin to appreciate that the words they know about *size* can be applied not only to individual objects, but also that words like 'big', 'bigger', 'small', 'smaller', 'more', 'less', etc.,[4] are used to describe or compare the sizes of *groups.*

Beginning to think about comparisons

This language of description and comparisons is important because with it children usually start to actually use concepts such as 'more' and 'less', 'bigger' and 'smaller', etc., in their practical activity.

When they are able to describe comparisons, typical children usually become able to express consequences and say things like "It's not big enough" or "I need more."

Even before they can count, they can usually make approximate practical judgements. Such judgements contribute to learning about numbers when children experience the same language of size being used alongside number words when they watch and listen to adults subitising and counting.

Many of our special children need much more experience of learning to notice changes and recognise and describe differences in practical activities.

 27.3 Online reading illustrates some examples of making comparisons and a lesson game. 27.4 discusses the language of comparisons.

But mathematical language can be confusing

When we use modelling talk, we need to be aware that the language of size and comparisons. As it crops up in everyday conversation or in questions it can be confusing even for the most able of our special pupils. Some examples include:

- *Sound-alikes* – 'won', 'too', 'free' and 'for' may seem silly examples, but there are many other sound-alikes that can be misinterpreted (e.g. add/had, weight/wait, pair/pear).

- *Different meanings* – sometimes words of everyday English have different meanings in mathematical contexts (e.g. whereas a 'takeaway' commonly refers to buying a pizza or curry, in a mathematical context it relates to subtraction; some other examples are 'even', 'answer', 'left', 'how (many)', 'order', etc.)

- *Precise listening to and understanding of grammar* – some statements or questions require precise hearing and understanding (e.g. word order – "That is bigger" or "Is that bigger?" – or small words like 'not' inserted in the middle of a phrase reversing its meaning) might easily be missed by a child.

We sometimes flit between words and phrases in ways that may confuse children, such as using a phrase like "You have two too many," or you might ask "What is the difference?" and whilst you may mean numeric difference, the child may answer, "That one is blue." In many circumstances, we are often unaware of children's language misconceptions, and since children themselves do not understand that they do not understand, they do not seek to clarify. For some of our special learners, one of our main aims is so fundamental that perhaps in the past it has been overlooked. Simply, we need to enable children to appreciate that there are words that describe size. Beyond that, of course, is the understanding that those words can be used to express comparisons of size and quantity.

 27.4 Online reading includes more about learning the language of comparisons

Notes

1 See references to Lacey and to Imray and Hinchcliffe in Chapter 23.

2 The cycle of learning processes rolls on as a wave – as described in Chapter 14.

3 Awareness of cause and effect (sometimes described as 'contingency awareness') has been discussed earlier in the book as a starting point for developing 'thinking'. It is important to recognise that active learning at this level is an important beginning for all children, but Routes for Learning describes how some PMLD children will be developing through this level for many years. Penny Lacey suggested that developing active contingent responses is an essential element of developing choice-making skills within learning about problem solving for PMLD pupils.

4 At the same time as they are learning this comparative language, they are also being exposed to learning number words through subitising – which will be discussed in a chapter of its own.

About number sense

Seeing number is an essential skill of life

This chapter will summarise what research has found about the development of *'number awareness'* in typical infants. It highlights a range of important perceptual skills that underpin learning about number that exists before counting. Newborns immediately notice when there is more than one thing and can also distinguish between small groups of up to four.

A human adaptation of a general biological skill

Similar use of size perceptions is common across the animal kingdom; for example, birds know how many eggs they have. But humans are the only species to develop a number system that connects perceptions to a thought system of names about ordered quantities (Butterworth, 1999).[1]

Number senses and special children

Though often taken for granted, these early perceptions have important functions for special children because they are practical parts of making sense of real-life events (Porter, 2010).[2] They are useful even for those who do not become numerate in the conventionally expected sense. Knowing more about number sense may be helpful to us in helping pupils to develop greater awareness and encouraging their curiosity and engagement in useful interactive learning.[3]

First perceptions

It seems that seeing connections between things and making comparisons is intrinsic within the infant's processes of looking, listening or touching. Most likely, an infant notices a group of four raisins as an entity, not as separate items, and will immediately subconsciously notice that it is different to a group of three raisins that is nearby. Just as if you were to see three people standing beside only two chairs, you would be very likely to register there are not enough chairs without actually counting.

These perceptions help children develop senses of quantity and to notice when things match, compare or change. They support the development of expectations or estimations useful for problem solving – and for most children they help them to learn that quantities have got names, called 'numbers'.

Every day you use it and refine it

Even as an adult, your intuitive perception of quantity is practised and guides your actions in so many ways, such as in all the choices you make when looking and choosing in the supermarket – you pick the hand of bananas that has about enough for you. When you get to the checkout, you select the shortest queue. As you pay, you notice there are not many pound coins left in your purse, so you select a note to pay with.

Neuroscience has observed number sense

Neuroscience has confirmed theories of innate number awareness, concluding that newborns already have brain circuits that are specialised in recognising how many objects there are in a group. Both Stanislas Dehaene[4] and Brian Butterworth[5] in books that survey the beginnings of mathematical thinking confirm that babies and other animals perceive spatial information in ways that enable them to compare the sizes of groups, and they also register surprise if the outcomes of small changes are wrong.

It has been established that initial perceptions of quantity happen in the left parietal lobe, which has roles not only in the visual perception system, but also in integrating other senses, notably touch and the use of the fingers.

The parietal lobe is where:

- Initial perceptions of small quantities are registered.

- Sensory activity of spatial perception is integrated – *including visual, tactile, kinaesthetic and auditory information.*[6]

What is our intuitive number sense like?

A *New Scientist* interview available online reports that Butterworth (1999)[7] believes that the activity in our left parietal lobe not only enables but also compels most of us to see the world in terms of number. In the article, he uses a metaphor to explain that we can't avoid instantly enumerating things any more than we can avoid seeing in colour. When we see a green leaf, we immediately grasp its 'greenness'; likewise, if we encounter three dots on a page, we straight away grasp its 'threeness'. Observing numerosity is innate – unless you are dyscalculic.

We need a bigger picture

When infants see groups bigger than four or five, they can't tell how many there are in the group. They often just say there are 'lots'. But they can often choose which is the larger of the two groups because they have a second intuitive number sense that deals with larger quantities that cannot be perceived exactly at a glance. Researchers have described this as an 'approximate number sense'.

We have two systems of number sense

Firstly, we have a precise system for exactly perceiving small quantities, which plays a part in our immediate practical life in terms of exactly recognising, comparing and matching small groups – but it is also the background from which children learn that quantities have got names, called 'numbers'.

Secondly, we have an approximate system that distinguishes proportional differences of larger quantities, which is important in our practical lives for making comparisons and estimations regarding bigger numbers. It is an essential part of practical problem solving, being the basis of rapid comparisons and estimations.

Levels of number sense

From perceptual beginnings to developing verbal and symbolic coding

Stanislas Dehaene is a neuroscientist who describes intuitive number sense as the biological beginnings of maths. He acknowledges the foundation processes begin with sensory information (including visual, tactile and auditory) in the brain's parietal lobe, which integrates visual and spatial thinking (2010).[8] However, to become ideas that can be expressed either in verbal language or symbolically as numerals, the perceptual number sense has to be connected to other brain circuits that we use to express conceptual thinking – and he suggests that thinking about number uses three coding systems that need to be integrated.

Firstly, using the parietal lobes:

■ *Quantity code* – visual, sound or touch images that are patterns of number sense

Subsequently using other brain areas:

■ *Verbal code* – spoken language, starting with number names

■ *Symbolic code* – representations and numerals

Our teaching and modelling should aim to illustrate and enable children to connect these three aspects of thinking.

In his review 'Making Sense of Number Sense', Daniel Birch (2005)[9] suggests that fleshing out the intuitive beginning of number sense is usually a byproduct of other learning. It is a broad process of life experience, so I suggest that, in addition to any specific individual teaching, practical and social activities – including problem solving and games that exercise sensory learning are the ideal circumstances for us to enhance children's awareness of number sense.

We need to:

■ Expose children to lots of sensory experiences of quantity that exercise their use of perceptual number sense.

■ Provide lots of modelling and opportunities for them to use language and representations.

As we engage in teaching number sense through life experience, there are factors to bear in mind that could help us be more effective. The next few chapters will look at some of these factors.

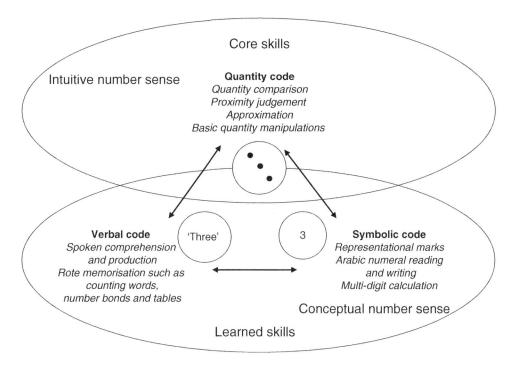

Figure 28.1 The brain uses three coding systems for number

Notes

1 Butterworth, B. (1999) *The Mathematical Brain*. London: Macmillan.

2 Porter, J. (2010) Developing number awareness and children with severe and profound learning difficulties. *SLD Experience* 57, 3–7; Porter, J. (2015) Using number in everyday life. In: P. Lacey et al. (Eds), *The Routledge Companion to Severe, Profound and Multiple Learning Difficulties* (pp. 316–323). Abingdon: Routledge.

3 As discussed in Chapter 15 on the processes of learning and the related online reading about the engagement profile advocated in the Rochford Review.

4 Dehaene, S. (1997) *The Number Sense*. London: Penguin.

5 Butterworth, B. (1999) *The Mathematical Brain*. London: Macmillan.

6 It is important to be clear that mathematical thinking does not rely on just the parietal lobe, nor is the parietal lobe just dedicated to number. Number sense informs other aspects of thinking, particularly verbal and symbolic coding that use other parts of the brain, and they work together to enable number sense to mature. Thinking about number requires flexible connection, as described in Haylock's pyramid (Chapter 18).

7 Butterworth, B. (1999) True Grit, interview by A. Motluk, *New Scientist*, www.newscientist. com/article/mg16321935-000-true-grit/

8 Dehaene, S. (2010) The calculating brain. In: D. A. Sousa (Ed.), *Mind, Brain, and Education* (pp. 186–188). Bloomington: Solution Tree Press.

9 Birch, D. (2005) Making sense of number sense – implications for children with mathematical disabilities. *Journal of Learning Disabilities* 38(4), 333–339.

29 An exact number sense for small quantities

When researchers like Starkey (1980)[1] first explored children's intuitive perceptions of quantity, they called them 'number sense'. At the early level, it is a bit of a misnomer, because they are at first only perceptual abilities, not initially a knowledge of number – though they are perceptions from which learning about numbers starts.[2]

Noticing numerosity

Noticing and remembering the nature of small groups is the absolute beginning of both making comparisons and learning that quantities have names. Newborns can distinguish two objects from three and possibly three objects from four. When groups are more than four in number, the infants cannot see differences. Even adults have similar limitations, and the range doesn't improve much with age, although the fluency with which perception is used, alongside patterning, and the ways it is connected to language[3] are usually improved by practice. This chapter is mainly about perceiving groups. In a later chapter, I will look in more detail at how children start to use their number sense to *name* quantities – subitising.

Dyscalculia

There is growing awareness that some otherwise able children have number sense problems. They cannot discern the 'twoness' or 'threeness' of a group, which means they do not develop a 'feel for number'. Though many of them use counting – which they have learned by rote – they find it difficult to think flexibly about numbers and to estimate or anticipate the real outcomes of changes. They are described as dyscalculic.

Though this book is principally written to relate to the learning of children with SLD or PLD – who are rarely given a diagnosis of dyscalculia – it is worthwhile to note that there is some overlap at the roots of learning.

29.1 Online reading contains more notes on the threads of number sense and dyscalculia

Exercising number sense

Recognising groups and being able to hold them in memory enables the child to connect the quantities that they see to the words that adults use to name them, and this process occurs in everyday experience – which we have to emphasise for our special people. Luckily, there are lots of opportunities for matching and sorting groups and matching words to their specific quantities in practical activity or social events and games.

 29.2 Online reading contains more notes on exercising number sense and using games

Noticing differences and reacting to changes

Noticing differences

In 1992, Karen Wynn[4] conducted a classic experiment using a puppet theatre with five-month-old babies. They watched puppets being placed behind a screen and then were surprised if the screen opened to show either more or fewer puppets than they had watched being hidden. She played this out with various combinations and concluded that as the babies watched, they formed ideas about what the outcome *should* be, and they were surprised if the result was wrong. This suggested to her that the babies actually had 'arithmetic expectations' about small addition or subtraction experiences. Other research that has followed reinforces Wynn's suggestions.[5]

Seeking and finding
Older children of 14 or 15 months also showed expectations, but with increasing accuracy. After they had seen up to three objects being hidden, they appreciated how many times they needed to reach into the bag to retrieve them – and would search hard if the last one could not be found. This led McCrink and Wynn[6] to propose that children could have mental representations of hidden things and could both keep track of hidden numbers and correspond their actions to things.

These researchers went out of their way to create situations that motivated children by using their curiosity and natural interest in things appearing and disappearing. This reinforces all of the suggestions I have made about teaching through practical activities and games. Many domestic activities include putting away, getting out or seeking and finding, and many games include hiding and revealing. In them, problem solving can be generated in motivating circumstances that need not feel like tests. Of course, the way adults behave, switching between modelling and provoking action, and the way they use language will be key to creating such challenging informality.

Expressing their understanding

Thinking back to the complications arising from language and grammar described in Chapter 27, some children might be hindered by language in expressing what they understand.

There is some more research that used motivating contexts that might prompt us to think about teaching approaches. In a series they called the 'magic experiments', Gelman and Gallistel (1986)[7] found that 2.5-year-old children who did not usually use mathematical words were able to understand problems and express comparisons by using the idea of 'winner' and 'loser'. This might give us something interesting to consider. Though those children are far from the cognitive age usually able to carry out subtraction, they do have a grasp of its outcomes when the situations are posed in contexts and language they can grasp.

Such informal situations could be a stepping stone for us to use. We might think in terms of using real things and creating circumstances in which pupils are challenged to anticipate outcomes within the range of their number sense. In this way, with our modelling, we might start to give them experiences of what words like 'more'/'less', 'bigger'/'smaller', etc., actually mean – as well as exposing them to number words being used alongside quantities they can see, etc.

Intuitive number sense is multisensory

Number sense is not just visual – children have sensory memories of touch and movement and they discriminate groups of sounds, such as drumbeats, or sequential movements (McCrink & Wynn, 2004).[8]

Sound and rhythm

The feel of a sound group 'da da da' is as distinctly different from 'da da da da', as are their visual counterparts. The same number sense limitations apply – it is easy to register three sounds, but difficult when there are more than four or five sounds.

Just as rhythm and intonation play fundamental roles in learning language, they contribute to establishing the awareness of linear sequence that underpins understanding the number line sequence, whilst time durations also link to the sense of magnitude, as discussed in Chapter 24 (Walsh, 2003).[9]

Blind people subitise sound patterns and represent them in movement. Sound patterns are rapidly connected to touch and movement experiences such as clapping or finger movement. They are naturally adopted by children and the fact that songs and clapping are traditional ways of learning number is no coincidence, but conventionally it is not much recognised in formal teaching beyond kindergarten. But music (and dance) is still a motivating learning force for adolescents and adults. We should recognise the power of rhythm, song and dance for older pupils by using songs, chants, stomps or beatboxing appropriately.

To improve our effectiveness as teachers, we should also know how to use rhythmic and tonal emphasis in our voices and make the best of the ways we use of our actions when modelling.

 29.3 Online reading includes links to Sounds of Intent – a useful resource for observing PLD progress. It is based on music, but is relevant to all communication and to reflecting the roots of maths

Movement and touch

Linear and sequential movement is part of the power of music mentioned above. It is also inherent in the processes and rhythm of domestic activity or games, such as stacking plates with attitude or swinging a swing ball with rhythm. Emphasising the movements of reaching, touching and placing and coordinating them with vocal modelling focuses attention. Teachers need to use the dramatic art that is necessary to create focus and draw students into echoing your modelling!

 29.4 Online reading includes some sound and movement activities that include experiences of number sense

Spatial perception and groups

When we are presenting or arranging stimuli, there are influences that affect the spatial perception of small quantities (in either visual, auditory or tactile channels). They will quite possibly affect children's judgements, so we need to be aware of possible disruption – or how we may use them to make things clear.

Visually, for example:

Figure 29.1 Mixed stars

(i) We tend to look for connected, manageable units we can quickly make sense of, such as small groups of differently coloured stars (Fig. 29.1), which are easier to calculate than the whole group at once.

(ii) Issues like proximity, similarity, etc., affect the way our mind seeks to make lines or groups. For example, in Fig. 29.2, we may see these dots as two and two ones, or as a three and one, rather than four.

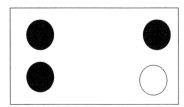

Figure 29.2 Two and two ones

(iii) As groups get larger, there can be more variations, and we may even switch between them. In fact, as we will see, this may be a skill to develop – seeing groups within groups.

Fingers and number sense

Fingers are our natural link between number sense and representation

The origins of representation

As previously discussed in Chapter 19, it seems likely that counting on fingers preceded using special words. They were the expression of our number sense before we had numbers. Butterworth tells us that number words and words for fingers or fists share the same roots in Indo-European and other languages. Think about it – we use the word 'digit' for either an individual finger or a numeral.

Neurological links

Brain research now tells us that the parietal lobe integrates spatial perceptions from the senses with our finger control. Neurologists who are interested in maths suggest that finger manipulation and shape making is a form of spatial reasoning that helps intuitive number sense extend towards:

1. Ideas about representing number

2. The structure of the number line

3. The genesis of using counting

Fingers are a natural element of learning number used by children in all mathematical cultures without being formally taught. Some even use fingers to represent quantities before they use the respective number names, and in formal education settings children will also use them even if it is forbidden.

Fingers – a link from intuitive to conceptual number sense

Using fingers to represent quantities is one of the first steps towards abstract representation – a bridge from intuitive thinking to conceptual thinking. The Dutch educators Fosnot and Dolk (2001)[10] noted how very young children develop an understanding of the idea of 'how many?' from experience of perceptual correspondences with fingers:

1. Fingers are first used to represent a one-to-one representation of individual items.
2. Fingers are then used to understand that finger movement and shape making can represent quantity beyond the limit of the intuitive number sense.

Observing typical children at play, we see them instinctively practice using their fingers, both consciously and subconsciously, in sensory play or in conjunction with songs and rhymes:

- *Initially they practice making manipulation fluent* – getting better at sequential movement or shape making.

- *Later they use them as tools for various purposes* – to match, coordinate sequences of words and objects, enumerate, count, remember or represent number.

- *Some* are able to extend from just representing small numbers to ideas, such as showing sequential increase, two-hand addition or folding-back subtraction.

With special pupils, however, we might need to model and promote the practice of finger manipulation and patterning at various levels, all of which occur usefully in practical life. We might need to:

- Enable them to develop hand movement and pointing

- Develop fluent finger manipulations

- Represent quantities – showing how many

- Track sequences – as used in counting

- Develop forms of hand calculation

A text box suggesting relevant hand and finger work and resources was included in the section about using fingers for thinking in Chapter 19.

Notes

1 Starkey, P. & Cooper, R. G. (1980) Perception of numbers by human infants. *Science* 210(4473), 1033–1035.

2 More recently, the term 'number sense' has been adopted by mathematics educators to refer to a framework of ideas that enable children to understand numbers and number relationships. Gersten and Chard describe it as children's fluidity and flexibility with numbers. Gersten, R. & Chard, D. (1999) Number sense: rethinking arithmetic instruction for students with mathematical disabilities. *The Journal of Special Education* 33(1), 18–28.

3 The connection to language occurs in a process called 'subitising', which is the subject of a forthcoming chapter.

4 Wynn, K. (1992) Addition and subtraction by human infants. *Nature* 358, 749–750.

5 Wynn's conclusions about babies' intuitive expectations depended on observing their surprised reactions. Later researchers have detected surprise by measuring eye gaze and pupil dilation, body movements and changes in sucking reflex responses.

6 McCrink, K. & Wynn, K. (2004) Large number addition and subtraction by 9 month old infants. *Psychological Science* 15(11), 776–781.

7 Gelman, R. & Gallistel, C. R. (1986) *The Child's Understanding of Number* (pp. 83–85). Cambridge, MA: Harvard University Press.

8 McCrink, K. & Wynn, K. (2004) Large number addition and subtraction by 9 month old infants. *Psychological Science* 15(11), 776–781.

9 Walsh, V. (2003) A theory of magnitude: common cortical metrics of time, space and quantity. *Trends in Cognitive Science* 7, 483–488.

10 Fosnot, C. T. & Dolk, M. (2001) *Young Mathematicians at Work – Constructing Number Sense, Addition and Subtraction*. Portsmouth, NH: Heinemann.

30 An approximate number sense

Larger quantities – approximate number sense

We often need to make practical decisions beyond the perceptual limitations of three or four objects. Consequently, we use a second number sense system that deals with larger quantities that cannot be perceived exactly at a glance. Researchers have described this as an 'approximate number sense'.

Many researchers are very interested in the role of 'approximation' in developing mathematical thinking because they see that it has a strong connection to using flexible thinking, which is problematic for dyscalculic children.

Some researchers have even found that children playing approximation/estimation games *before* they have more formal lessons improves their performance in the later session.

It would be very interesting to see if motivating perception games would be a good exercise to help special pupils, perhaps using games like the 'Colour Dots' app by Ellies Games, which is a pointing game.

 30.1 See online material on how making comparisons stimulates mathematical thinking

A sense of proportions

Approximate number sense does not give us precise numeric answers, but distinguishes between quantities by making proportional comparisons. It has many practical uses; for example, the foraging primate can use it to choose the tree that has the most fruit, and likewise we can use it to estimate if we have enough biscuits for a group of visitors. In yet another sensory dimension, hearing lone footsteps can tell us that someone is coming, but hearing many footsteps together warns us there are a lot of people behind us. All of these examples illustrate that even before we use 'numbers', we use comparisons for real-world judgements and problem solving. So, developing awareness and refining the approximation sense is useful in our students' practical lives. Even without reaching the levels of using number, it helps them to compare, choose and estimate.

Approximation

Take a look at the squares in Fig. 30.1.

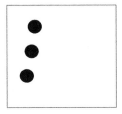 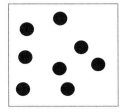 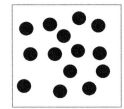

Figure 30.1 Spot squares

Chances are that you knew instantly how many dots there were in the left-hand square – but it took a little longer with the middle square, and you probably had to count them. You almost certainly needed to count in order to know the number of dots in the right-hand square, but it was quite easy to see that it has more than the others, because you are capable of making choices on the basis of *approximate perception*.

The distance effect

Young children can do this, choose the biggest pile – but only if there is a very big difference. A typical five-month-old can notice there is a difference between 20 and 10 (ratio of two to one) – but not between 15 and 10 (ratio of three to two). Over time, typical children get better at this, and by nine months of age, they can see the difference between 8 and 12 things.[1] Experiences that enable this refinement are obviously important to everyone in order to make comparisons and estimations. Most typical children will develop this without teaching, but children with special needs need us to provide relevant experiences.

Somebody has been eating my biscuits

Using our memory of approximate perceptions might eventually alert us to the fact that someone else is taking a biscuit from our tin each day. But it wouldn't do so immediately if the tin were quite full because differences have to be significant for us to notice.

Why approximating and comparing quantity is important to developing number

Flexible thinking

In the general population, children who are good at making visual comparisons usually become able to use flexible approaches to number problems.

Dehaene (2010)[2] wrote: "The ability to approximate gives children an intuition for problems."

Children who are good at approximation perform well when learning about maths, both as infants and later in school life, because approximate number sense helps them develop strategies for managing quantities (Gilmore et al., 2010; Halberda et al., 2008)[3]. It is the basis of matching, comparing and choosing to make judgements (e.g. recognising when things are the same or which is the largest quantity in a practical problem or the big number in a subtraction – and working on from there).

Improving approximate number sense

In one large study, Halberda and colleagues (2012)[4] found that the approximate number sense usually refines simply from everyday experience without any specific teaching through the school years and into adulthood.[5] This is a good sign because it means that it can be improved. Consequently, researchers have suggested that there is good reason for finding ways to teach about the approximate number sense.

Ideas about maths develop even before numbers

Lauren Resnick (1992)[6] suggests that seeing approximate differences and comparing groups is a starting point for mathematical ideas. As children encounter comparisons of groups and hear words like 'big', 'lots', 'more', 'less', 'most', etc., they are experiencing concrete reasoning that illustrates ideas about:

- Differences

- Increase/decrease

- Part and whole schema

These are usually mathematical ideas children understand even before they understand numbers.[7]

Experience of them is intrinsic to understanding about number relations and operations, and giving children exercise in noticing and using these ideas in practical contexts may stimulate their useful senses of differences, comparisons, etc.

Some experiences for exercising approximation and comparisons

- Observing when groups of things are the same or different.

- Realising when there may not be enough or there are too many.

- Working out how to change these – knowing when more are needed.

- Perceiving when a pattern is incomplete (e.g. when we notice empty spaces in the chocolate box).

 30.2 Online reading contains a more extensive list of experiences for excercising approximation and comparisons

Notes

1 But even as adults, we never become completely accurate – we may be able to discriminate that there are differences between groups of 12 and 14 or 100 and 115, but naming them exactly is not possible.

2 Dehaene, S. (2010) The calculating brain. In: D. Sousa (Ed.), *Mind, Brain and Education – Neuroscience Implications for the Classroom* (p. 183). Bloomington, IN: Solution Tree Press.

3 Gilmore, C., McCarthy, S. & Spelke, E. (2010) Non-symbolic arithmetic abilities and achievement in the first year of formal schooling in mathematics. *Cognition* 115, 394–406; Halberda, J., Mazzocco, M. M. & Feigenson, L. (2008) Individual differences in non-verbal number acuity correlate with maths achievement. *Nature* 455, 665–668.

4 Halberda, J., Lya, R., Wilmerb, J., Naimana, D. Q. & Germinec, L. (2012) Number sense across the lifespan as revealed by a massive internet based sample. *PNAS* 109(28), 11116–11120.

5 Peaking at around age 30.

6 Resnick, L. (1992) From protoquantities to operators: building mathematical competence on a foundation of everyday mathematical knowledge. In: G. Lienhardt, P. Putnam & R. Hattrup (Eds), *Analysis of Arithmetic for Mathematics Teachers* (pp. 373–420). Hillsdale, NJ: Erlbaum.

7 Resnick used the term 'protoquantitive schema' to describe the early 'prototype' ideas about quantity that children have before they understand about numbers, whilst other researchers such as Geary described them as relational concepts (i.e. ideas about relationships).

31 Understanding comparative value – including exchange and money

Within our community of special children, there is a wide range of levels of ability relating to the use of money. Some children with profound difficulties never handle their own. Even for the many with SLD who can participate in shopping experiences, the exact use of money is problematic since it requires levels of counting and mental arithmetic they may not have mastered. There may be a few more able pupils who do use money to pay for everyday items independently, but they still have a lot to learn about greater values and money management.

 31.1 Online reading references some teaching resources for more able young adults

Pre-monetary starting points

The roots of understanding about obtaining and exchanging things you may value happen a long time before children are numerate. There are social starting points to understanding about money. They start at pre-numeric levels, but have a lot to do with making comparisons and estimations. We usually learn them incidentally in life, but we need to work on them with our special pupils. They are principally about understanding the ideas of *exchange* and *comparative value*. These ideas are relevant to children in many social interactions even before they can use money. As with many other aspects of learning, they will occur at different levels with different children of different abilities, but their importance changes and grows if children go on to use money in shopping. The following sections outline some aspects of social knowledge that children need to know before they can understand the use of money.

Awareness of exchange

One of the ways children develop awareness of social action is through the simple acts of giving and taking. These are basic human necessities as well as sources of pleasure – they include the pleasure of receiving and of giving, as well as experiencing the consequences of exchanging things, which often leads to thinking about value.

Awareness of reward and payment

Through social action, we can introduce children to experiences of reward or receiving payment. These can occur in classroom management[1] or in motivating contexts of enjoyable and leisure experiences or winning or losing in games.[2]

For rewards, we can use direct pleasures that give immediate gratification or tokens that can be objects, stickers, etc., to be collected or exchanged for things children value. There are many positive things for them to learn, such as the enjoyment in earning a reward, spending it, saving to accumulate and so on.

Paying to receive

Realising other people need something from you in return is the other side of the equation – appreciating the need to pay in order to receive – which leads to the question: have you got something to offer or exchange? Or, when shopping, do you have something to pay with?

Awareness of value

Any things or events that are important to the child are the starting points for teaching them to understand about 'value'. We can use reward trading and bargaining as a way of introducing them to comparative value, enabling them to appreciate that their things have comparative worth and there needs to be a matching process – bargaining – to meet other people's expectations.

Thinking about money

When children appreciate the dynamics of exchange and value, they will be better able to appreciate the dynamics of shopping. However, dealing with the values of coinage and calculation still presents considerable difficulties that often stand in the way of independence for them.

Taking care of your money, putting it in a safe place and keeping and being aware when the purse is full and when it is getting empty are basic lessons. Comparing how much you had and how much you spent may be an approximation for some, but it is valuable to learn to be aware when you are nearly spent up.

Realistic use of money

Traditional ways of teaching about the value of money usually start with young children adding the values of small coins together. But this is problematic for most SLD pupils whose counting and addition skills are limited.

For a start, it's unrealistic – small coinage on its own does not buy practical things. Using small-denomination coins in role play also often leads to using teaching resources that present unrealistic examples (e.g. a chocolate bar costing 5p). So most schools with SLD pupils take a practical life skills approach. Instead of struggling to calculate the value of small change, they engage pupils in developing comparative ideas about what kinds of things can be purchased with 50p, £1 and £2 coins and £5 notes. In fact, this is what many of us do in shops rather than tendering exact money – we give coins or notes that will cover the cost and wait to receive change.

These experiences can happen in school with either role-play shopping or a tuck shop. Experience can be extended by doing real shopping. Children might be involved in budgeting choices, anticipating and comparing and choosing which items to buy. This leads to thinking about what is too expensive or good value (e.g. two for one offers, etc.) or what could be bought if we save until next time or if we share with another person.

In the shop, students might do the picking and paying. Sometimes they make their own selections when spending their own money. Remember the advice of Penny Lacey and, where possible, let them solve their own problems. If they try to buy more than they have funds for, remember it's OK to let them make mistakes – it's a vivid way to learn. Shop staff are usually understanding – and you can hover nearby to step in if needs be.

When pupils get good at these estimations, they can move on to learning about combinations of coins. This is not to say that those who develop addition skills or comparative skills with apparatus like Numicon should not work on the specific value of coins.

> **31.2 Online reading includes some suggestions about work on experiencing the value of coins**

Comparing coinage

Learning to identify coin names is a rote activity. Comparing coinage value is not easy and language is fraught with possibilities for misconceptions; for example, which coin is bigger – 50p or £1? The sizes of the coins do not reflect their value. *So, asking which is 'bigger 'or 'smaller' may be confusing.*

When practising in classroom games, it is most desirable to use real coins, because plastic replicas do not have the same feel. Touch is an important element of choosing coins. Think about it – you initially select pound coins from your pocket without looking at them (selecting from a feely bag of different coins is a good activity).

> **31.3 Online reading includes a game for experiencing comparative values of coins**

Larger values

Though many of our pupils are dependent on adults when it comes to purchasing larger or expensive items, it is desirable to work with them on understanding comparative value and budgeting – appreciating what can be afforded, what needs to be saved for, etc.[3]

The advent of cashless shopping

Developing thoughts about value and budgeting may become even more important for some of our young people. The introduction of contactless cards may soon be a way of widening opportunities for spending decisions for them. There is already a contactless, pre-paid debit card called 'Go Henry' that can give children the freedom of independent spending, but has various parental controls, via a mobile app, so that funds can be safeguarded. Some families and organisations already use it and have special arrangements for accounts to continue beyond the usual age range.

Older pupils are often fascinated by flicking through shopping catalogues or fliers. In particular, the Argos catalogue is a great resource for looking at or cutting up in order to develop discussions or games about affordability.

These print resources can be used as the basis for teaching sessions creating opportunities for work on value and comparisons, such as creating collages of things pupils like or making wish lists or present lists by physically cutting out or by photographing into a story board app.

Notes

1 It can also occur in behavioural training contexts – but the nuances of delivering rewards in behaviour programmes is subtle and dependent on many individual factors beyond the scope of this book.
2 Gelman and Gallistel's 'Magic Experiments' found that children 2.5-year-old children could often understand or even predict the general outcomes of events when they were asked to think in terms of winner and loser.
3 Teaching resources from the Money Advisory Service cover issues like this, particularly for people with disabilities who may enjoy a degree of independent living (see online reading for a link).

32 Number is like space

The ideas of number and space are linked

Stanislas Dehaene tells us that cultural intuitions that link numbers with space and the concept of a 'number line' have deep intuitive roots in the brain (2008).[1] He also tells us that for most children "number is like space" (2010).[2] According to Dehaene and others, brain research has observed brain activity that links the working of areas of the brain that are used for quantity to areas that are engaged in spatial judgements, including the area that controls the fingers. More recently, researchers have added experience of time intervals to the list of influences (Walsh, 2003).[3]

Children's earliest experiences of moving themselves in space and time, tracking, sequentially scanning or touching arrays of objects and itemising fingers all contribute to them developing both spatial awareness and awareness of sequence. Spatial experience is essential to forming linear ideas of size and understanding progression of increasing or decreasing values.

The number line

The mental number line is a feature of thinking in all cultures. Whilst the direction of the number line varies for different cultures,[4] even tribes with limited number language instinctively map numbers spatially along a line. It is the way we all learn to relate size to order.

Can you see it?

Around 14% of people are readily able conjure up a visual number line to see in their mind's eye and use it for thinking about order and size (Seron, 1992).[5] However, for the majority, the number line is usually more of an intuitive feeling we reference unconsciously. But if needs be, we can think hard about it – sometimes gazing into space or nodding our heads – and we can cross-reference it to finger representations or draw it. As our ideas about number mature, we can envisage larger numbers, but not exactly (see online reading 32.4).

As teachers, we need to think of ways of promoting children's sensory learning and actuating the actions, ideas, vocalisations and visualisations of a number line. We have already touched on the importance of multisensory 'visualisation' in previous chapters when we discussed developing awareness of object permanence and recall. It is important in many ways and we will return to this in the later chapter on counting when we discuss the abstract processes of recalling and counting things that have been hidden.

 32.1 Online reading contains more about the mental number line

Developing ideas about lines

Typically developing children will follow sequences of action and sound that, when related to pointing at or placing objects, helps them establish the idea of the one-to-one sequencing of number (McCrink & Wynn, 2004).[6] They also naturally arrange objects as part of their play processes and may connect linear arrangements of small quantities to the language of 'ordinal number' when they hear it modelled by adults. If children with very special needs don't make the connections between ideas and language so easily, we need to emphasise them. Modelling needs to use every sensory mode – not only visual arrangements, but also physical movements, tactile experiences, sound patterns and mark making. There are many activities that involve making sequential arrangements, starting as simply as clapping games and progressing through linear distribution to connecting tracks and board games, which have the potential to teach us some important lessons, such as:

1. Finding the place of a particular number on a line

2. That value increases as you progress

3. That you can compare size from the position on the line

One downloadable computer game specifically designed by neuroscientists to strengthen number line activity is called 'The Number Race' (http://thenumberrace.com/nr/home.php).

 32.2 Online reading contains more ideas about linear activities

The connection to fingers

I noted earlier that the area of the brain used for spatial perception also connects to controlling the fingers. The connection between fingers, space and number interests psychologists and neuroscientists like Butterworth, who has written extensively about it (Butterworth, 1999).[7]

The idea of a number line begins with small, perceptible quantities. Pica et al. (2004)[8] observed that, usually around the age of three, young children (who can name small quantities just by looking) "exhibit an abrupt change in number processing." The changes are prompted as the children come to understand about the finger activities they have been learning and they integrate related ideas, such as:

- Each count word actually refers to a precise quantity.

- Sequencing fingers in a line and pairing them one to one with number names gives them the number (which they may already know by 'subitising' – just looking).

- Appreciating that the specific finger shape represents the whole number.

These realisations allow the appreciation that the fingers can be both symbols for representing quantity *and* a tool for finding quantity.

Using fingers creates the idea of a line that will eventually take children beyond the limits of small numbers. As they appreciate the connection between fingers, linear objects and counting words, they can begin to understand that the number line can extend even beyond their fingers and is the beginning of a continuous system.

Pattern seeking and number naming

When items are not linear, it seems that intuitive pattern seeking or shape recognition plays a large part in quantity perception. When items are close together, even in random arrays, there are patterning tendencies that we tend to notice, such as: 'two' objects appear as a linear pairing; 'three' objects tend towards a triangular shape; and 'four' objects tend towards a quadrilateral shape. Beyond four, the random shapes created are less distinct and groups are harder to identify. Pairing objects within groups is a common strategy for speeding up recognition.

Practicing group perception

These processes can be affected by perceptual tendencies such as colour matching, spatial proximity, etc., which we have discussed in previous chapters. Consequently, there is a need to work on practicing discrimination in all sensory modes, and this process involves participating with adults, tracking sequences and actions, handling and pointing, practicing seeing, hearing and matching small groups and patterns, copying, identifying what is the same or different, comparing and choosing, arranging and rearranging things. Such activities need not necessarily require numerical responses from less able students – but adult counting provides good modelling. All of these activities are good preparations for developing the recognition skills that become the process of subitising – which is the subject of the next chapter.

32.3 Online reading contains examples of activities with small groups

The interplay of perception and language

In all of the cases mentioned above, it is evident that both linear and group identification are dependent on sensory and perceptual skills. But translating and communicating about perceptions is also full of difficulties that arise from the complexity of language about comparisons we have discussed earlier.

Classic examples famously occurred in Piaget's conservation of number experiments. Children watched a linear group being changed by an adult via simply spreading objects wider, and when they were asked, "Is it more or less?" some children would say it was more. Piaget concluded that the children did not appreciate that the group had stayed the same. Many researchers, however, suggested the question was confusing and the children were making common sense conclusions, because when the group was spread out it looked more! Actually, these kinds of misconceptions are common in everyday life and can confuse learning (or assessment). So it is very important to be aware of possible pitfalls when we are modelling and work towards dealing with them.

Everyday experience

Linear and patterning experiences are often encountered and practiced with maths equipment such as abacuses, bead strings, cubes, boards, rods and Numicon. However, a great deal of background experience in recognising lines and patterns occurs in practical activity, play and craftwork, all of which provide real opportunities for us to model the use of mathematical language.

When the number gets bigger

The mental image of a number line initially grows due to a combination of number sense and finger counting (Griffin, 2002).[9] Its evolution is supported by linear activities with small numbers and the use of language alongside them. It is important because it is a foundation that leads children to a mental construct of the progression of larger numbers. But as numbers get larger, they are not possible to perceive exactly, and long lines of objects or marks are not helpful to learning. So spatial representations of larger numbers need to take on other forms. Similarly, it is difficult to identify the quantity of a large random group.

Larger numbers are mostly beyond the general remit of this book for children with SLD, but later chapters will look at ways to make groups perceptible using grids. Readers who work with children who do use larger numbers will find advice and resources for using number grids, ten frames, hundred frames, Cuisenaire, etc., online or in some of the resource books I recommend when I touch on dyscalculia (e.g. the number sense interventions book by Jordan and Dyson, 2014).[10]

32.4 Online reading contains more information about when the number gets bigger

Notes

1 Dehaene, S., Izard, V., Spelke, E. & Pica, P. (2008) Log or linear? Distinct intuitions of the number scale in Western and Amazonian indigene cultures. *Science* 320(5880), 1217–1220.

2 Dehaene, S. (2010) The calculating brain. In: D. A. Sousa (Ed.), *Mind, Brain, and Education* (pp. 193–195*).* Bloomington, IN: Solution Tree Press.

3 Walsh, V. (2003) A theory of magnitude: common cortical metrics of time, space and quantity. *Trends in Cognitive Science* 7, 483–488.

4 There is an element of cultural influence; for example, the line tends to follow the direction of writing. In Western cultures, larger numbers are to the right, in Arabic and Hebrew to the left.

5 Seron, X. et al. (1992) Images of numbers, or when 98 is upper left and 6 sky blue. *Cognition* 44, 159–196.

6 McCrink, K. & Wynn, K. (2004) Large number addition and subtraction by 9 month old infants. *Psychological Science* 15(11), 776–781.

7 Butterworth, B. (1999) *The Mathematical Brain*. Chapter 5. London: Macmillan.

8 Pica, P., Lemer, C., Izard, V. & Dehaene, S. (2004) Exact and approximate arithmetic in an Amazonian indigene group. *Science* 306, 499–503.

9 Griffin, S. (2002) The development of math competence in the pre-school and early school years: cognitive foundations and instructional strategies. In: J. M. Rover (Ed.), *Mathematical Cognition: A Volume in Current Perspectives on Cognition, Learning and Instruction* (pp. 1–32). Greewich, CT: Sage.

10 Jordan, N. & Dyson, N. (2014) *Number Sense Interventions*. Baltimore, MD: Paul H. Brookes Publishing.

33 Subitising – connecting perception with number

Stepping from intuition to ideas

Subitising – immediate naming of number

If your number sense is working well, when you look at a die you don't need to count – you can shout out the number the moment it stops rolling. 'Subitising' is the name of this skill. The word is drawn from Latin for 'sudden'. It is the skill of making immediate perceptual judgements and naming the size of the group without counting. It is a combination of number sense and naming and is a skill we take for granted, but it is important for children because it begins to establish knowledge of numbers even before counting.

Subitising starts before counting

Most children learn to use subitising by copying adults applying names to small groups of one to three. For example, they notice that adults say, "You have two feet and two shoes, but only one hat." Typical children soon start to use the specific number words they have heard for particular quantities of things when they see them. It's a useful skill, and as we have seen, there are often finger and physical actions accompanying it.

Early ideas of comparison stem from subitising

Being able to 'just see' what a number is without conscious effort may seem to be a very simple skill. In fact, it is so basic that it is not even mentioned in the National Curriculum programmes of study. It is, however, the essential preamble for mathematical ideas. It is so important that, without it, practical mathematical or numeric thinking is completely disrupted.

Douglas Clements (2014),[1] following the work of Fuson (1992),[2] describes how subitising is the first introduction to *cardinality*.

The cardinal number is the number that represents the size of the group

Clements and Fuson explain that cardinality is an important idea, because it is about *representing quantity*, (i.e. relating to questions like 'how many?'). *Cardinality* is also essential in order to make comparisons so as to think about ideas such as 'more' and 'less' – which are the beginnings of practical maths, as well as arithmetic and all that follows. Learning subitising is the first way we use cardinality when we name numbers by looking, even before we can count.

Subitising plays a role in developing counting

Subitising happens before counting, but it also plays an important role in learning to count meaningfully (Treacy & Willis, 2003).[3] The last number name used in a counting sequence is the *cardinal number* and it represents the size of the set. But a very young child whose mind is engrossed in the sequence of pointing actions and words may not realise that significance. In fact, research suggests that even though they use cardinal numbers in other circumstances to describe groups, children don't usually appreciate cardinality *in counting* until around the age of four (Nye, 2001).[4]

Subitising contributes to that realisation because, during the initial stages of developing their counting skills, children are often surprised when the sequential count they make coincides with the same number that they have already noticed by subitising. This often happens when they are making a one-to-one correspondence with fingers, as does the realisation that numbers get bigger or smaller when one is added or removed. Starkey (1995)[5] has observed that, in these circumstances, subitising helps children to realise that 'counting' is not just a pointing and word game, but is a process they can use to find out 'how many', so subitising and counting integrate to make counting become meaningful (see figure in online reading).

 33.1 Online reading includes a figure that illustrates how number sense and practising counting occur on parallel paths, with subitising linking them

The place of subitising in the curriculum

Clements (1999)[6] suggests that the emphasis on counting in conventional curricula leads to subitising being relegated. There is often insufficient work on the subitising that should precede and proceed alongside counting. The curriculum drive to teach the performance of counting overrides the value of making estimations. This is a tendency that reduces children's experience of flexible thinking about approximation and comparisons. It leaves them dependent on the laborious, linear processes of counting. As a consequence, many children, but particularly those with dyscalculia, have a poor 'feel for number'. They lack understanding about the relationships between numbers and are unable to anticipate and estimate outcomes or think of strategies that use comparisons to solve problems.

 33.2 Go to online reading for Chapter 29 for notes about dyscalculia

Children with SLD may not have been given a diagnosis of dyscalculia, but they are delayed in counting. They also find it difficult to communicate about comparisons of numbers. Taking these together, it seems reasonable to suggest that all I have said about developing number sense – and extending that to exercise of subitising – will be of value to them.

The place of subitising in life

Subitising is often experienced in everyday life, such as quickly saying how many apples are left in the bowl, how many squares of chocolate we've been given or making quick random judgements in life or games (e.g. how many coins were tossed on the table?). It contributes to strategies we use for living because it enables quick and precise communication. There are a growing number of good resources for focused teaching (e.g. spot cards, manipulatives, etc.), but the motivation found in real-life contexts and the momentum of games are the most powerful opportunities for teaching.

Don't miss opportunities

Clements and Sarama (2014) suggest that the easiest and most effective way you can contribute to children's learning about small numbers is to use the words as frequently as possible in everyday actions. For example, instead of just giving them cups to put on the table, include the observation – "Can you put these three cups out?" It need not be artificial – simply use number words whenever it makes sense. This echoes suggestions in previous chapters about using mathematical language in everyday problems as advocated by Penny Lacey.

Levels of subitising

Clements (1999)[7] suggested that subitising works at two levels:

1. **The initial 'perceptual' level** – recognising matching and naming quantities
2. **The 'conceptual' level** – when children use the idea of subitising for mathematical purposes

We might add:

3. **The 'symbolic' level** – when seeing or even just saying numerals connects to ideas of quantity

Perceptual subitising

This is the level at which many of our special pupils will be functioning. Some will step beyond it, but others with more profound difficulties will remain on this bridge between perception and mathematical knowledge.

 33.3 See online reading for thoughts on pre-symbolic subitising and thinking

Perceptual subitising is the first step from an intuitive number sense, as the parts of the brain that observe quantities make connections with areas for verbal language. It is limited biologically to small numbers – beyond four it needs to have patterns . It is useful for practical purposes of naming, saying how many, starting to compare and using numbers. It is the experience from which children learn about cardinality and it is a preparation for the strategies we all use for finding larger groups.

Some ideas that are useful to include in games and activities in order to teach perceptual subitising might include:

- Experiencing and learning the general idea that quantities have names.

- Cardinality – the idea that any particular quantity has a consistent name.

- Identifying different arrangements of the same quantities – objects or images.

- Identifying some larger patterned groups.

- Playing rapid looking and saying games of chance.

- Seeing a quantity first and checking it by counting.

- Subitising patterns of sound or actions.

- Subitising visuals with sound patterns (Barth, 2005).[8]

- Trusting judgement – without counting.

- Developing the idea that when a quantity changes, the name changes.

- Understanding number words have useful purposes for counting and for comparisons.

 33.4 See online materials for ideas about teaching perceptual subitising

Conceptual subitising

When numbers get a little larger
When groups get larger than four, they move out of the range of immediate perception, so that children will either have to count them all or find further

strategies in order to identify them. In her excellent online article, Jenny Back (2014)[9] provides us with some examples, like the ones below, that illustrate the kinds of ideas that need to be applied alongside perceptual subitising in order to recognise larger groups. She also describes some useful card games for numerate pupils.

Different ways of subitising groups of five

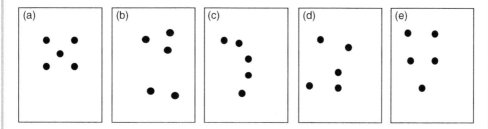

Figure 33.1 Different ways of subitising groups of five

A. A traditional or playing card/dice arrangement, most of which use the symmetry of parallel pairs to make instant recognition possible without other mental strategies.

B. Here we may instantly recognise subgroups of two and three, and most of us can apply the number fact of 'two and three makes five' very quickly.

C. A linear arrangement that is likely to prompt counting, though in this case some people might be affected by the curve and either separate the dots into groups of two and three or see the two and count on '3, 4, 5'.

D. A random arrangement, with more ways to form the subgroups. This could be considered to be the most difficult of the examples.

E. Encourages seeing a four and a one make five. Patterning sometimes leans towards the domino format of two small numbers for rapid addition.

The examples illustrate that, even for adults, the recognition of quantities between five and ten begins by perceiving small sets. But when the groups are randomly spaced it often requires additional work.[10] For example, to solve these examples, we may see a small group and 'count on' or see two groups and use rapid addition or decide to resort to counting. Writers like Resnick (1989)[11] recognise that exercising such decisions and strategies of comparison and combination contributes to flexible mathematical thinking.

So conceptual subitising is about more than recognising and naming – it is about *using the idea* of subitising and knowing you can use the patterns along with counting or addition to work with larger groups.

Conceptual subitising and special children

More able special pupils may progress to this stage if they are able to use counting and have ideas of addition. It involves recognising patterns of small sets and using them for thinking; for example, a child might explain, "I saw three and counted another two," or, "I saw a three and a two and it's five."

There are an increasing number of maths recovery programmes that, even for more typically developing children, advocate the use of iconic images, as well as apparatus such as Numicon, ten frames, soroban, Slavonic Abacus, etc., and of course computer programs.

About teaching conceptual subitising

Some ideas that are useful to include in games and activities in order to teach conceptual subitising might include:

- Seeing parts and wholes – patterns that are parts within larger groups.

- Making larger numbers by combining groups.

- Appreciating the idea of combining or separating groups.

- Breaking down and rearranging sets in different ways (decomposing and recomposing).

- Using iconic images and resources such as pictures or ten frames.

- Being aware of using counting.

- Knowing counting is a process used to find how many.

- Appreciating size and comparisons – equating/finding the place of a group on an empty number line.

- Being aware of 'counting on' to find how many.

- Finding whole numbers by using either 'counting on' or combining the parts they see by using some number knowledge.[12]

- Making smaller numbers by removing a group.

- Learning some addition facts.

- Describing comparisons numerically (e.g. acknowledging which number is bigger, etc.) by using number names.

> **Jelly bean discrimination**
>
> Finlay enjoyed an art session (inspired by the book *How Many Jelly Beans*) as he worked with Mrs Green. They used three different colours of sticky spots to make a paper plate look as if it had groups of jelly beans on it (there were ten altogether). Later, he also enjoyed defining the groups again by matching the real jelly beans to the spots. He probably enjoyed it more because he was told that, if he could guess which was the biggest group, he could eat them at the end.

 33.5 See online materials for ideas about teaching conceptual subitising

Symbolic subitising

The brains of adults, fluent in the use of symbols, shift seamlessly from seeing a numeral to an appreciation of its related quantity. We can even compare quantities just by hearing names. Vice versa, the instant we see a group of things, we can relate its magnitude to its verbal name or numeral. Hearing number names or seeing numerals actually creates activity in the number sense areas of the brain. These instant connections between three forms of thinking – visual quantity code, verbal code and symbolic code – were discussed in the chapter on number sense and illustrated in Fig. 28.1.

The meaning of numerals

Many of the number sense resources that are coming onto the market for mainstream schools quickly move their attention to subitising directly from the symbolic code of numerals. Perhaps they assume that if the child can say the name, they also know that the numeral *represents* a quantity. But this is not the case for many children with special needs, who are not fluent abstract thinkers – even those who recognise numbers may not really appreciate their meaning. They still need experiences that extend awareness of symbolic representation and make meaning of numeral recognition.

Connecting images and symbols

Ansari (2010)[13] suggests children learning about numerals may benefit from stimulating experiences where both symbolic and non-symbolic formats *are presented together*. There are many ways to connect numerals to their corresponding quantities in games. Ansari particularly suggests that linear number games are good contexts, for presenting numerals and movement. We can also make opportunities in real activities with real things, such as clothes peg lines or stepping stones.

Ansari recommends that, in all those contexts, the ensuing conversations (and *modelling*) should emphasise not only making judgements about equality, but also commenting on inequality, why things are different and how they could be changed. All of these ideas coincide with my earlier suggestions about teaching children through the medium of real problem solving.

If you do have pupils who understanding the connection between symbols and quantity and yet still require reinforcement programmes, you may find 'Maths Recovery' or resources such as those produced by Ronit Bird useful to you. There are references and links to these in the online reading for this chapter after the section on ten frames.

 33.6 Online reading on symbolic subitising

To summarise

Subitising is an underestimated skill that links children's images from an intuitive number sense to ideas of size and value (cardinal number) and the use of counting words. It contributes to making counting meaningful. It is important to teach and use subitising alongside counting.

Notes

1 Clements, D. H. (2014) *Learning and Teaching Early Math, Second Edition.* Chapter 2. New York: Routledge.

2 Fuson, K. C. (1992) Research on whole number addition and subtraction. In: D. A. Grouws (Ed.), *Handbook of Research on Mathematics Teaching and Learning* (pp. 243–275). New York: Macmillan.

3 Treacy, K. & Willis, S. (2003) A model of early number development. In: L. Bragg, C. Campbell, G. Herbert, & J. Mousley (Eds.), Mathematics Education Research: Innovation, Networking, Opportunity: Proceedings of the 26th Annual Conference of the Mathematics Education Research Group of Australasia (Vol. 1, pp. 674–681). Melbourne: Deakin University.

4 Nye, J., Fluck, M. & Buckley, S. (2001) Counting and cardinal understanding in children with Down syndrome and typically developing children. *Down Syndrome Research and Practice* 7(2), 68–78.

5 Starkey, P. & Cooper Jr, R. G. (*1995*) The development of subitizing in young children. *British Journal of Developmental Psychology* 13, 399–420.

6 Clements, D. H. (1999) Subitizing: What is it? Why teach it? Teaching Children Mathematics 5. Reston V.A. NCTM, http://gse.buffalo.edu/fas/clements/files/Subitizing.pdf

7 Clements, D. H. (1999) Subitizing: What is it? Why teach it? Teaching Children Mathematics 5. Reston V.A. NCTM, http://gse.buffalo.edu/fas/clements/files/Subitizing.pdf

8 Barth et al. found that adding audio beeps could improve five-year-old children's subitising. Barth, H., La Mont, K., Lipton, J. & Spelke, E. (2005) Abstract number and arithmetic in preschool children. *PNAS* 102, 14116–14121.

9 Back, J. (2014) Early Number Sense, https://nrich.maths.org/10737

10 Using pattern perception to discern small groups within larger ones is an important element in helping children to understand that numbers can be made up of parts. Such understanding also underpins ideas about the possibility of combining *or* partitioning groups, which is necessary to understanding what is happening in practical or symbolic calculations.

11 Resnick, L. (1989) Developing mathematical knowledge. *American Psychologist* 44, 162–169.

12 Typically, children develop such skills as they pass through early levels of the National Curriculum, so we would only expect children who are passing beyond the range of this book to master these processes.

13 Ansari, D. (2010) The computing brain. In: D. A. Sousa (Ed.), *Mind, Brain, and Education* (p. 216). Bloomington, IN: Solution Tree Press

34 Counting

As easy as one, two, three, we take counting for granted. Like reading, it is one of life's basic skills. Many people seem to assume that the skill of 'counting' gradually happens through practising the counting words. Those of us who work with children who have SLD become aware that this is not the whole case.

Generally, teachers are very conscious of the sub-skills that young children need to learn before they read or write. A wide range of pre-reading and pre-writing materials are available to help develop constituent literacy skills. Most maths schemes, on the other hand, give only cursory acknowledgement to the *sub-skills of learning to count* and move very quickly to expecting children to use counting for answering questions. Though there is research information available about how children learn to count, there is less practical guidance for teachers that illustrates either the constituent parts of the processes of counting or the background roles of 'subitising' discussed in the previous chapters.

Is counting a simple skill?

Coordinating actions

As infants learn to speak, delighted adults use rhymes, stories and songs to teach them the number names and are soon rewarded by children repeating them. Proud parents relate that they can count to three, and later, ten and so on. There is, however, much more to meaningful counting than repeating sounds. In fact, it involves doing many things at once.

In the complex language of the psychologist:

> When counting the child must co-ordinate the production of two continuous active sequences, saying the numerlogs (number words) and producing pointing actions, whilst concurrently co-ordinating the pointing with a set of spatially distributed objects.

These requirements, accurate production of number words, plus, their co-ordination, in time with pointing, and in space with objects, *allows considerable scope for error.*

(McEvoy, 1989, emphasis added)[1]

Understanding language

To add to the physical difficulty, even the way we use the names of numbers is confusing. Without giving a second thought, adults use number names in different ways:

- *They are 'ordinal'* – when they are used as labels, they represent a place in an order (e.g. 'six' on a ticket means the sixth seat in the row), but when used in a *counting sequence*, ordinals are temporary tags.

- *They are 'cardinal'* – when they are used as labels to represent quantity (e.g. 'six' on a packet means it contains six biscuits).

- *They are 'nominal'* – when they are used as names, often with no direct connection to quantity (e.g. the number on a 44 bus route).

Confusingly, we even interchange these usages as we are counting; for example:

- We point at each item and say, "One, two, three," as if they were the names of the things we were pointing at.

- But on reaching the last item, we change our meaning because we know our last word describes the size of whole group. Do children realise the difference?

Awareness of the purposes of counting

Even when the physical actions and words of counting are learned, that is not the end of it, because to be useful, all that word production and itemising needs to be done with a purpose that the child understands. But research on what children think about counting shows that many pre-schoolers don't realise what counting is for. They think of it as a game in itself, a social activity or performance done with adults – they don't initially see it as a *tool to ascertain quantity* or that numbers are a system to use to describe order and size (Munn, 1997).[2]

 34.1 See online reading on awareness of the purposes of counting – the findings of Penny Munn

Even though they perform the rituals, it takes time to come to understand the purpose of counting. It happens as described in the previous chapter:

1. As first, they practise the processes of counting; *and*
2. They realise connections between their counting results and the perceptions of subitising.

If typically developing pre-school children don't initially see the important purposes that are beyond the playful facade of the counting, how will children with learning difficulties fare? Jill Porter highlights the importance of SLD children learning to appreciate the *purposes* of counting and learning *to use it* in an excellent summary (Porter, 2015).[3]

Five counting principles

Because we have the misconception that counting is one simple skill, adults are often frustrated when special pupils struggle. To relieve the frustration and find ways to teach, we need to understand that counting is a collection of skills and knowledge that have to be synchronised.

Gelman and Gallistel (1978)[4] described five principles that are necessary for accurate and meaningful counting. The first two are about how to carry out a verbal count, but the last three are connected to meaningfulness.

Principles related to how to count

- The one-to-one principle
- The stable order principle

Principles related to meaningfulness

- The cardinal principle
- The abstraction principle
- The order irrelevance principle

The principles help our teaching

As we count, all the principles work together, but knowledge of the specific parts of the counting process can help us refine our teaching:

- It enables teachers to focus on sub-skills and set realistic challenges. With more specific knowledge, we can provide support to ensure that the child learns specific skills, rather than fails by not being able to coordinate all the parts of counting to produce the right answer.

- Being aware of the detail of counting processes, the teacher will be able to recognise teaching opportunities in everyday situations and games (e.g. they will see the value when there is opportunity for pointing, tracking, keeping tally, matching, stacking, visualising, comparing, naming, etc.).

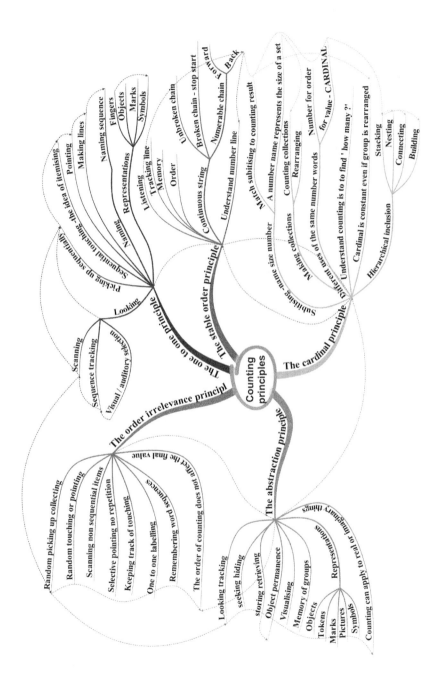

Figure 34.1 The principles of counting

- When working with a mixed-ability class, knowing the parts helps us to accommodate the needs of individuals as they share experiences together. For example, in a game there can be appropriate goals for each student:

  - Lorna may be learning to look and track.

  - Stephen may be at the level of pointing to itemise.

  - Shafiq might be including word order in his responses.

  - Ruth might be able to track the score during each turn on her fingers or score card.

  - Jaycee is acting as croupier – controlling each turn and calling out the score.

- Together, they can play a game of chance with an adult who enables each to participate at their own level, keeping the flow going with a skilful use of variable challenges, support, prompts and cues. All the pupils are involved together and made aware of winning or losing, which motivates learning.

Teaching the parts of counting

Principles related to how to count

The one-to-one principle
This requires the understanding that, when counting, each item has its own name tag and is only counted once. It is the basis of enumeration.
   Developing this principle at its most basic requires:

- Starting with eye pointing and tracking (pointing is a key skill in both social communication and mathematics).

- Drawing attention and sharing attention to single items.

- Touch pointing.

- Keeping track – following across sequences physically or mentally tracking which items have already been attended to or counted.

When it begins to be numeric, it includes:

- *Name tagging* – summoning up and applying distinct number names one at a time.

Problems and teaching related to the one-to-one principle
It has been particularly noted that difficulties with object tracking contribute to Down syndrome children's counting inaccuracies (Gelman & Meck, 1983).[5] Sella (2013)[6] and Porter (2010)[7] have noted they are more likely to skip items than double count.

Focusing on one-to-one itemisation leads to enumeration

Games or practical activities often provide motivating opportunities to practise the one-to-one principle by pointing, distributing, matching and enumeration. Even for more able pupils, developing fluency is of benefit because it frees brain processing power for other parts of counting.

At early counting levels, children are often vague about their pointing – they wave their fingers in the general direction and need to learn to point precisely. They let the rhythm of speech dominate the speed at which they count, and lose one-to-one correspondence, miss items or double count without noticing.

Some ideas about teaching related to the one-to-one principle

All that has been said in previous chapters about developing manipulation and movement skills is relevant, such as arranging sequences of objects, counting objects into containers, counting claps, skipping, counting sounds and counting regular and irregular spaced objects or sounds.

 34.2 See online reading for more ideas about working together on the one-to-one principle

The stable order principle

Numbers are sequential names used in fixed order

The oral string it is not the whole process of counting, but nevertheless children cannot begin to count until they can perform some of its chain.

Developing this principle at its most basic requires:

▪ Coordinating sequential sound making

▪ Remembering – actions and sounds

When beginning to be numeric, it includes:

▪ Learning the sequential list of number names

To progress, it requires:

▪ Being able to start at any point in the sequence

▪ Being able to go forwards or backwards in the sequence

Problems and teaching related to the stable order principle

Working memory

Children acquire counting words and order first through memory and later using pattern. The long string of words that represents the number line is a challenge to learn because we can only hold information in our minds for a short time. When you want to remember a telephone number, you need strategies to do so – it's likely you use chunks and intonation.

 34.3 See short-term memory limits in online reading

All children take time to achieve a stable counting order. To teach special children, we need be aware of the stages that typical children pass through and the strategies for memory they naturally use, because they need to be the framework of our teaching and modelling for our special pupils.

The familiar song of counting
Most of our special children use these early phases:

1. Initially, children imitate *strings of sound* – 'onetwothreefour' – that use rhythm from breath, pattern and intonation. It is no coincidence that there is a cultural heritage that naturally strings these short phrases into chunks of number rhymes and songs. There are stages in how children move on from the continual string. We should observe where the child is and model appropriately.

2. Gradually, children start to recognise individual words, but can still only recite them as an '*unbreakable chain*' starting from the beginning. Being able to pause then continue, or even to stop and continue – learning to use a '*breakable chain*' – is an important next step to realising that the chain is made up of individual points and step towards realising that counting is more than recitation. This is the point where connecting counting to cardinality begins.

3. The next steps are to be able to start from any point – '*the numerable chain*'. It will be necessary for children to understand this before they will be able to use 'counting on' as an addition strategy.

4. Then they become able to say numbers from any point in either direction counting up and down – '*the bi-directional chain*'.

Some ideas about working together on the stable order principle
Throughout these developments, sound and actions play their parts – they are inherent in the traditions that make number songs memorable. But that does not preclude us from finding appropriate use even with older students. The same devices are used by adults in mnemonics and found in chants, or even in advertising. Gesture, rhythm and intonation make the chain memorable, but also provide punctuation and intonation that emphasise where meaning is (e.g. a rising tone and gesture at the last number emphasises cardinality).

 34.4 See online reading for a more ideas about working together on the stable order principle

Principles related to the meaningfulness of counting

The cardinal principle

This requires understanding that the final number used when counting represents the size of the set. Since it requires applying the two previous principles, it therefore matures after them.

Developing this principle at its most basic requires:

▦ Understanding that numbers represent quantities

When beginning to be numeric, it includes:

▦ Seeing the connection between subitising and outcomes of counting

▦ Using counting to find out how many

To progress, it requires:

▦ Understanding using it to count on or to carry out addition

Cardinal numbers are used at an earlier level than counting
Even before they can count, some very young children do appreciate the idea that numbers represent the size of groups. For example, infants can tell you that they have seen three pigs at the farm or had two sandwiches, and they name small groups just by looking (subitising). *But* it takes some time to connect:

▦ The idea of cardinality that they use when subitising

▦ To the idea of *using it when counting*

Nye (2001)[8] suggested typical children use *cardinality in counting* around the age of four. The evidence suggests that some children with Down syndrome also achieve its use, but at a delayed rate. Sella (2013)[9] suggested their development is hampered by tracking difficulties and poor visual discrimination of small groups. Which supports the suggestion of the previous chapters on the importance of teaching visual discrimination and manipulation skills, as well as the importance of children using subitising and counting practice in parallel.

Cardinality – connecting naming and awareness of value
In early counting sessions, children will recite numbers along a row of objects, and if they manage to synchronise the tally, they can arrive at the correct number. Despite their apparent success, you might still might suspect they don't really appreciate the cardinal principle, because if they are then asked 'how many?', even immediately after they have just finished counting, they often start counting again. So it seems they don't realise that the cardinal value of a group remains the same. It seems they see 'how many?' as a prompt to count (Fuson & Hall, 1983).[10]

Similarly, if there is pause after counting a group – and you put some more items down and say 'how many now?' – they will go right back and count them all instead of 'counting on'. The ability to count on is a fundamental strategy, but it depends on being sure about cardinality.

Confusion about purpose

It also seems that they do not realise the different purposes we use number words for, which I mentioned earlier:

1. Ordinal – to track the sequence
2. Cardinal – to name the size of the group

Children may not be aware of these distinctions, so when we ask even a typical four-year-old to count a row of five objects, they may count them correctly and say that there are 'five', but they often will think that the fifth object is the five. Perhaps they are interpreting each number word as a proper name of each item. So, for that child, the word 'five' is just the name of the last object, not the entire group (see Fig. 34.2). How can we help them be aware of the value of the group?

Hierarchical inclusion

There is another idea that is closely related to the cardinal principle, and it is illustrated in the lower part of Fig. 34.2. It's called 'hierarchical inclusion', and the idea is that any larger number includes – contains – all of the numbers that come before it.

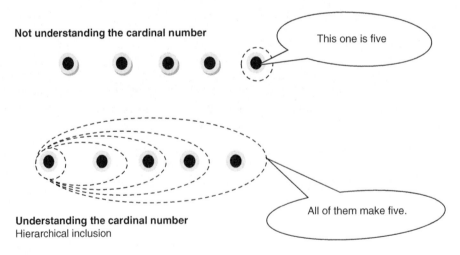

Figure 34.2 The cardinal principle

Counting for cardinality

Appreciating the importance of cardinality in counting – realising counting is not just a verbal performance or a game – is an important milestone in a child's mathematical development, because:

(a) It is when they realise that counting is a useful tool for finding out *how many*.

(b) It can take their number range beyond the limits of perceptual subitising.

Some ideas about teaching related to the cardinal principle

Counting to find out

The simplified description I gave of 'hierarchical inclusion' gives us clues about ways to teach cardinality. We should be modelling ways of counting that show that the *number includes everything that's been counted.*

It's easy to see how a child who counts along a row of five objects might simply think only the last one is called 'five' and the others are not included. So here is another way to illustrate it: if you start with a row of five plant pots or beakers to count, as you pick each one up and say its number, stack it onto the next. Continue so that they end up nested together in one stack, which you call 'five altogether' using a rising intonation to emphasise the result.

Lots of commercial manipulative maths apparatus such as Linking Cubes or Numicon tiles can show cardinality, but there are also are endless motivating opportunities in practical activities and games that not only involve stacking or nesting as I described, but also making collections and comparisons, counting things into containers, gathering all counted items together into one pile or building a tower.[11] Always conduct such work with physical gestures – and create mistakes and problems to provoke pupils' thinking.

 34.5 See online reading for more ideas about working together on cardinality.

The abstraction principle

Understanding that counting can be applied to any collection – real or imagined
Developing this principle at its most basic requires:

- Understanding things still remain the same when they are out of sight

When beginning to be numeric, it includes:

- Understanding that quantities can be remembered – or imagined or counted – even out of sight

To progress, it requires:

- That thinking can be used for planning

Remembering or counting things you can't see is the beginning of thinking abstractly about numbers – it begins with visualisation. I have noticed that if I ask someone how many radiators they have at home, they often pause and look upwards as they think, which suggests they are using visualisation to go on a journey around their house. Some even nod their heads or move their fingers as they interpret their mental imagery – which may just be a mental feeling.

Adults understand that they can count things that are not physically present, and they can use that same skill to remember, or even imagine, quantities of things. All of that is very useful – and it is a life skill even for our special children. But early in life, even typical children can only count real things that they can see or touch. Can we help children visualise?

Some ideas about teaching related to the abstraction principle
These notes are expanded in the online reading.

The abstraction principle is about exercising thinking about things that are not there, which begins with appreciating object permanence and developing visualisation through many *games and activities that involve hiding and revealing to exercise memory.*

We also represent our thoughts and our memories by making representations – and even typically developing children use fingers and actions, objects, mark making, etc., as forms of thought to represent quantities they have in mind.

 34.6 See online reading for more notes and ideas about working together on the abstraction principle

The order irrelevance principle

Understanding the order in which items are counted is irrelevant; the same cardinal value will be reached so long as the stable order is used and none are left out. This principle requires knowledge about all the previous four principles.

Developing this principle at its most basic, it requires:

■ Developing understanding of the conservation of number

When beginning to be numeric, it includes:

■ Being able to maintain a count of random arrangements

It is necessary to be conscious of this principle in order to be able use counting as a flexible tool, particularly when items are not in rows or if they are rearranged. It is related to understanding that the size of a group remains consistent however it is arranged (conservation of number). It is confidence in that consistency that enables us to override misperceptions that may confuse us when spatial changes make things appear bigger/smaller. It is therefore related to our ability to make comparisons using numbers.

Some ideas about teaching related to the order irrelevance principle
We need to work together on activities that illustrate counting irregular arrangements:

- Illustrating number name tags are temporarily given for the purpose of counting.

- *Ideas about the conservation of number* – illustrating that the physical arrangement and spatial order of the counting does not affect the quantity.

- *Subitising practice and checking.*

 34.7 See online reading for more notes and ideas about working together on the order irrelevance principle

Notes

1 McEvoy, J. (1989) From Counting to arithmetic. *British Journal of Special Education.* 16(3), 107–110.
2 Munn, P. (1997) Children's beliefs about counting. In: I. Thompson (Ed.), *Teaching and Learning Early Number* (pp. 9–19). Buckingham, PA: Open University Press.
3 Porter, J. (2015) Using number in everyday life. In: P. Lacey et al. (Eds), *The Routledge Companion to Severe, Profound and Multiple Learning Difficulties* (pp. 316–323). London: Routledge.
4 Gelman, R. & Gallistel, C. R. (1978) *The Child's Understanding of Number.* Cambridge, MA: Harvard University Press.
5 Gelman, R. & Meck, E. (1983) Preschoolers' counting: principles before skills. *Cognition* 13, 343–359.
6 Sella, F., Lanfranchi, S. & Zorzi, M. (2013) Enumeration skills in Down syndrome. *Research in Developmental Disabilities* 34(11), 3798–3806.
7 Porter, J. (2010) Developing number awareness and children with severe and profound learning difficulties. *SLD Experience.* 57, 3–7.
8 Nye, J., Fluck, M. & Buckley, S. (2001) Counting and cardinal understanding in children with Down syndrome and typically developing children. *Down Syndrome Research and Practice* 7(2), 68–78.
9 Sella, F., Lanfranchi, S. & Zorzi, M. (2013) Enumeration skills in Down syndrome. *Research in Developmental Disabilities* 34(11), 3798–3806.
10 Fuson, K. C. & Hall, J. W. (1983) The acquisition of early number word meanings. A conceptual analysis and review. In: H. P. Ginsburg (Ed.), *The Development of Mathematical Thinking.* New York: Academic Press.
11 Tower building has one weakness as a strategy – kids find it such fun to knock it down, which destroys the number.

35 Calculation and big ideas

Informal calculations

Life is full of calculations, even for young children and our special children, who can show anticipation of changes in small quantities. These are informal mental calculations that happen in practical situations, such as identifying 'not enough' or 'I need more'. They are relevant in our special curriculum because they are processes of approximation and choice making that are used to solve problems in everyday life. Some of our pupils will need to continue learning at such early practical levels, and we have discussed the importance of learning to make comparisons, approximations and estimations in previous chapters. Other pupils may well start a journey towards more numerical levels, so we need to know about how children begin to understand about addition and subtraction.

Ideas about changes

Practical skills and experiences of making comparisons, etc., play parts in developing mathematical thinking. In Chapter 30 (on approximate number sense), I discussed three sets of practical ideas that Resnick (1992)[1] suggested children have about quantities and relationships even before they use numbers. They are:

■ Comparisons

■ Increase/decrease

■ Part and whole schema[2]

All mathematical knowledge evolves from them, but they are essentially ideas born from practical observations and are important to practical life for all children, even those who are working at pre-'numerate' levels. Whilst typical children explore them with ease, we need to promote them in our special children. We can emphasise them in every form of activity, and experience of them spawns more thinking about practical calculation.

📝 **35.1 There is an example of practical calculation, developing experience in a life skills context in the online reading**

Some more big ideas

There are other notions that evolve in children's minds about sequence, order, size, how things change, etc. Mathematicians often describe them as the 'big ideas of maths' because they provide the foundations for thinking in mathematical ways,[3] which Fosnot and Dolk (2001)[4] describe as 'mathematising'.

Most descriptions in the literature about the big ideas refer to numerate levels of thinking. Even though many of our very special children are pre-numerate, some big ideas are still relevant to them, because the ideas have sensory roots and practical implications in real-life activities. They are important in practical activity, counting and calculation and give us ideas about things children need to learn.

Some big ideas that are important in the development of practical or numeric maths for special children

1. **Understanding there are things**

   - *Object permanence* – this is not usually thought of as mathematical, but it is impossible to know anything about number, expect constancy of groups or notice changes without it.

   - *One-to-one correspondence* – this is the basis of practical matching, mental itemising and enumerating with fingers – as well as being a precursor of making practical comparisons.

2. **Understanding there are numbers**

   - These are names that are used to describe sequence or size.

3. **Understanding there are patterns of change**

   - *Things happen sequentially* – this is the basis of practical organising and ordering, which will lead to the idea of the number line.

   - *Regular intervals* – sequential actions can be evenly spaced, and equal sizes/ values repeated.

   - *Increase and decrease* – size gets bigger when something is added, and smaller when part is removed.

4. Understanding there are regular rules

- *The number line*:

  - Numbers are arranged in sequence on a number line – each number has its consistent place.

  - Increase – each step along the number, the line gets bigger by one.

  - Decrease – each step back along the number, the line gets smaller by one.

- *Cardinality*

  - Numbers are names tell us how many there are in a group.

  - Using the number line tells us how many there are altogether.

- *Comparison*

  - One-to-one correspondence can be used to compare sets.

  - Numbers can be used to compare by value and order.

- *Conservation* – so long as nothing is added or taken away, the number of items remains the same, even if they are rearranged.

- *Hierarchical inclusion*

  - Because numbers progress sequentially by 'one', any number actually contains all the numbers that have come before it.

- *Whole and part relations*

  - Splitting and combining groups.

  - Numbers can be combined to make larger numbers.

  - Big numbers can be broken down into smaller parts.

  - Small numbers can be made up – by adding to them – to equal larger numbers.

  - Complementary numbers – if three and two make five, then two and three will also make five, etc.

The ideas are elements of number, but also elements of all the practical experiences that we incorporate in the activities and games that we use as contexts for teaching.

Addition and subtraction

Children may not be ready for numeric calculations until they have integrated their understanding of subitising with counting, *but* there are many circumstances in everyday life where we can teach children about the practical effects of gaining and losing. For example, experiences involving giving and taking, collecting and distributing and also games where winning by accumulating or losing by gradual depletion until there is nothing left all generate strong responses and are important aspects of life maths to practice and communicate about. Helping special children shift from purely practical levels towards 'thinking' about addition and subtraction requires some understanding of how typical children develop ideas.

Foundations of ideas

Children's first understanding of addition and subtraction begins through those practical experiences. As children learn to appreciate and anticipate the effects of accumulations or reductions, aspects of the big ideas coalesce in their minds. They are the building blocks of practical arithmetical processes. Whilst some special children may step towards understanding them as thought processes, other children will remain at concrete, practical levels. It is useful for teachers to understand the phases of development so that they can pitch teaching for either of these groups.

Practical foundations of addition

Linear addition

Initially, addition and counting are intrinsically linked because counting is in fact progressive addition. Early experiences of addition spring from appreciating the ideas of 'one', 'another' and 'make more'. The number line is a key visual and physical resource. It can come in many guises – it may be a homemade cardboard template to use with cubes at the table, it may be stepping stones across the playground or a computer game like 'The Number Race', developed by Stanislas Dehaene's colleagues.[5] The essence of a simple number line is moving along it step by step, and it is the basis of many games. Steps can be single for pupils who are still developing the count sequence or larger jumps determined by the throw of a die, etc. Many teachers will use a number line on which children can draw jumps.

Bead strings are good number lines to make or buy. One – called 'Sum Thing' – is double strung so groups will stay in place until they are slid along. Other strings have colour changes every five beads that makes number groups easily perceptible.

Rods, bricks and blocks all lend themselves to linear addition and making differences clear, such as:

- Matching groups against a number line or template.

- Making comparisons or making groups equal by measuring the rods or connected bricks side by side.

- Experiencing complementarty numbers – making the same number in different ways (e,g. five a can be made from three and two – or four and one, etc.).

Ronit Bird's 'Dyscalculia Toolkit' adds more to most of what I have said here. It is also a resource book with game ideas and photocopiable resources. Its appendix gives good advice on manipulatives. She points out that all kinds of things in all sizes and shapes can be counters. Things like clothes pegs can be pegged into groups or make lines, and paper clips can be linked. She particularly likes the glass nuggets sold for flower vases. Everyday resources are cheap and effective. She reminds us that changing the nature of counters is valuable and fun.

Change by joining

Early on, children understand addition as 'change by joining'. Its first stages involve drawing items together and combining groups. Even without counting these experiences, including the language we use to describe growth is useful to many pupils in order to see the effects of practical addition. For those who are using number, seeing groups being joined together is a good message about what addition actually is.

The idea grows wider as children experience the extension of their finger shapes or collecting things together to make progressively larger groups. Adults guiding speech during these activities can use key vocabulary, describing processes of combination and increase – the meaning of words or phrases such as 'put another', 'together', 'add to', 'make more', etc. all need to be learned. Our commentary can help children anticipate changes and encourage them to estimate.

Readiness for numeric addition

Griffin (2002)[6] tells us that when children have developed two systems – subitising as a means of identifying and comparing groups; and counting objects by matching with their fingers – they are equipped to work on practical numerical addition. Typically, around age four, children are still most reliant on the subitising, but by age six, they have integrated the systems so that they can equate the groups they see to a mental number line.

Obviously, lots of work on estimating and counting collections is beneficial to developing and integrating the two systems. The age ranges suggest that only a minority of our special pupils will master numerical addition, but there are some schools who may have a few who will work at this level.

Phases of learning the process of addition

Learning about addition passes through a number of phases that typical children move naturally through, but it is useful for teachers of special children to be aware of them and their order, so that we can both present and model problems in relevant ways and appreciate children's learning steps.

Three stages of doing addition by counting that children usually pass through by age were described by Butterworth (1999)[7] – they are progressively abstract:

1. *The union of two sets – sometimes described as 'count all'* – is a collecting process. If they are given two groups of objects to add, even if they have

already counted out each set, when they combine them they *count all the items again.*

2. *Counting on* – when children are able to use the broken chain level of counting or understand the cardinal principle, they are ready to carry out addition by *counting on.* If presented with two groups, they count the first set and then continue the count onto the second.

3. *Counting on from the largest* – when they are able to recognise which is the largest of the two groups, they can use a more efficient method, combining subitising and counting. They say the name of the largest group and then count on the second.

4. *Using whole and part understanding* – realising that numbers can be combined to make larger numbers, children may develop the ability to retrieve number bonds from memory – *patterning apparatus like ten frames and Numicon is useful for illustrating and practising.*

Hands and calculation

It is interesting to note that the sequence of strategies that children naturally develop to carry out hand calculations are mirrored by the stages of addition described above. Hand calculation starts with making whole sets to count all and gradually moves to quicker ways – saying numbers and counting on.

It could be useful for teachers to base modelling of finger counting on the phases that are natural to children and perhaps mimic them when modelling with objects or manipulative equipment.

 35.2 See online reading for a fuller description of the development of hand calculation

Foundations of subtraction

Just as we are fascinated and motivated by gaining things, we also have a natural desire to protect what we have. Consequently, we are alerted to losing things and have an innate interest in tracking decreasing quantities. These fascinations are part of our survival instincts and are essential practical life skills for all of our special pupils. Teachers need to provide experience and model vocabulary related to reduction in everyday activities and games (e.g. the vocabulary of separation and decrease might include 'take away', 'less', 'fewer', 'none/some left', 'finished', 'used up', 'no more', 'gone' and 'none'). It is interesting to note that the idea of 'less than' is much harder to understand than 'more'. In addition, it is useful to remember that Gelman and Gallistel (1986)[8] showed that young children found it easier to understand problems that were about 'winners' or 'losers'.

Forms of subtraction

Taking away

It is useful for addition work on the number line to also draw children's attention to the decrease effect of taking away – and that physical experiences of things being deducted, eaten, etc., result in depletion.

The simplest processes of subtraction – change by taking away – may initially seem simple to understand, as does the outcome of having 'less', or even 'none left'. But observing what is happening may be more confusing for children than we think because the answers are often arrived at in different ways:

- Taking some away – and counting the remainder – *the clearest way*

- Separating a group and counting the remainder

- Counting back as objects are removed

In addition, expressing the effects is rather more complicated than describing the positive outcomes of addition. For example, questions such as 'how many are left?' or 'how much less?' are more grammatically complicated because they contain both positive and negative elements.

Other, more complex forms

Subtraction also occurs in other ways that may also involve some confusing language for children. The online reading contains graphic representations that may be useful to bear in mind if you are modelling with manipulative equipment.

 35.3 Online reading includes graphic representations of the different forms of subtraction

Comparisons

We have already noted that making practical comparisons is one of the funda-mental processes and uses of mathematics, and children have ideas about it even before they use numbers. But moving from making practical choices to describing outcomes involves some potentially confusing language.

To describe a comparison, we have to judge how much more or less the groups represent, or work out the 'difference'. Those processes can be confusing because, when you make one statement, there is also an inverse, so questions arising from the same circumstance may be framed in different ways:

- How many more?

- How many less?

- What is the difference?

A child is more likely to complain, "It's not fair, he's got more than me!" rather than, "I have less!" because they have greater difficulty understanding 'less than' statements than 'more than' statements. This suggests that it is important for our activities and guiding language to work on helping children understand the equivalence of these two statements.

The inverse of addition

Sometimes subtraction is phrased as the opposite of addition. For example, if there were three cubes on the table, a question might occur like, "How many *more* do I need to make five?"Adults might easily see the answer can be arrived at by counting on from three or counting back from five, but the language may be confusing for children.

Complement of a set

When there is a mixed group of items, sometimes questions occur like, "How many are not black?"

These examples illustrate how language is crucial, especially when we consider the communication difficulties of our children. We can see how careful we have to be at pitching language, observing responses and watching for the clues in our language and actions that pupils use.

A note about multiplication and division – fractions

Multiplication[9] and division or fractions do not enter the formal curriculum until mainstream children are able to work at later cognitive levels than this book relates to. However, there are precursors to those processes that may be relevant to our pupils' practical lives, which will particularly happen during processes of collecting and distribution.

The roots of multiplication are in experiencing the practical rates of growth that are created by repeated addition or doubling. These effects can be encountered, for example, in making equal rows or piles or collecting small numbers of items from a number of different people and ending up with a lot.

The roots of division and fractions relate to the changes created by distribution or halving or sharing into parts. Experiences like distributing items from a collection to a number of people, dividing a pizza or giving out biscuits evenly are all practical challenges of division.

One resource that may be useful for teachers who are working with pupils bridging into the National Curriculum are the 'Bridging the Gap' pages produced by Birmingham Special Schools and available through the Dame Ellen Pinsent School website. They have also put Wave 3 materials online, which are very useful lesson ideas. They also have excellent Pinterest pages, under the heading 'BirminhamSENMaths'.

📝 **35.4 See online materials for Bridging the Gap links**

Notes

1 Resnick, L. (1992) From protoquantities to operators: building mathematical competence on a foundation of everyday mathematical knowledge. In: G. Lienhardt, P. Putnam & R. Hattrup (Eds), *Analysis of Arithmetic for Mathematics Teachers* (pp. 373–420). Hillsdale, NJ: Erlbaum.
2 Resnick called these ideas 'protoquantitive schema'; others have described them as 'relational ideas'.
3 But there is no definitive list of 'big ideas' because they blur into each other in different ways across the range of levels and mathematical applications.
4 Fosnot, C. T. & Dolk, M. (2001) *Young Mathematicians at Work – Constructing Number Sense, Addition and Subtraction* (pp. 10–13). Portsmouth, NH: Heinemann.
5 The Number Race. INSERM-CEA Cognitive Neuroimaging Unit, www.thenumberrace. com/nr/home.php
6 Griffin, S. (2002) The development of math competence in pre-school and early school years: cognitive foundations and early strategies. In: J. M. Rover (Ed.), *Mathematical Cognition: A Volume in Current Perspectives on Cognition, Learning and Instruction* (pp. 1–32). Greenwich, CT: Information Age.
7 Butterworth, B. (1999) *What Counts*. New York: The Free Press.
8 Gelman, R. & Gallistel, C. R. (1986) *The Child's Understanding of Number* (pp. 83–85). Cambridge, MA: Harvard University Press.
9 When multiplication is first taught in mainstream schools, sometimes teachers treat it as successive addition. But this is a matter of controversy, because whilst this works for whole numbers, it does not work for fractions – and so later on in children's maths careers it causes conceptual difficulties.

Index